TIKI
WITH A
TWIST

TIKI WITH A TWIST

75 COOL, FRESH, AND WILD
TROPICAL COCKTAILS

Lynn Calvo with
James O. Fraioli

UNION
SQUARE
& CO.

NEW YORK

UNION
SQUARE
& CO.

NEW YORK

Text © 2024 Lynn Calvo
Photography © 2024 Union Square & Co., LLC

ISBN 978-1-4549-5446-0
E-book ISBN 978-1-4549-5447-7

For information about custom editions, special sales, and premium purchases, please
contact specialsales@unionsquareandco.com.

Printed in China

2 4 6 8 10 9 7 5 3 1

unionsquareandco.com

Editor: Caitlin Leffel
Designer: Renée Bollier
Director of Photography: Jennifer Halper
Photographer: Sarah Jun
Food Stylist: Kaitlyn Wayne
Prop Stylist: Maeve Sheridan
Project Editor: Ivy McFadden
Production Manager: Kevin Iwano
Copy Editor: Terry Deal

Illustrations by sini4ka, and
Yuliia Khvyshchuk/Shutterstock.com

TO MY FATHER, JOHN, AND MY MOTHER, MILLY,
FOR THEIR ENDLESS LOVE AND SUPPORT
AND BECAUSE THEY ALWAYS SAID,
"NEVER GO STRAIGHT, ALWAYS GO FORWARD."

CONTENTS

INTRODUCTION

When I was a child, my grandpa Angelo, a World War II veteran, proudly displayed the hula girl tattoo emblazoned on the inside of his right forearm. "Make her dance!" I often cried. He flexed, and away she went.

Many servicemen, including my grandfather and novelist James Michener, returned from the war with romantic stories of the South Seas. As a result, the Polynesian presence in Western pop culture soared. Michener's tales served as the inspiration for *South Pacific*, the Rodgers & Hammerstein musical that premiered on Broadway in 1949. But a decade and a half beforehand, Louisiana native Ernest Gantt had unveiled Don's Beachcomber Café, America's first Polynesian-themed restaurant, in Hollywood. Soon after, Victor Bergeron opened the doors of the first Trader Vic's location. Debate raged between the two men over who had invented the infamous mai tai, but the tiki craze flourished, and other popular drinks, such as the Zombie and the Scorpion Bowl, soon shared the limelight.

The Polynesian influence on American pop culture peaked during the 1950s, making its mark on architecture, cuisine, and music—particularly the Martin Denny Orchestra. Denny, an American composer, became known as the father of exotica, a musical genre that celebrates tiki culture and combines the musical traditions of faraway tropical locales: bongos, congas, and Cuban jazz rhythms. Les Baxter, Juan García Esquivel, and Arthur Lyman also composed exotica music, and you can hear their work in the soundtracks of many movies of that period. Tropical mania waned for a time, but in recent years, the tiki craze has returned. Today, the revitalized Polynesian vibe is going just as strong as Old Spice or the Twinkie. Backyard bars and fruit cocktails abound.

But years ago in the Caribbean, when Cruzan rum sold for $1.89 a liter and islanders regarded clothing as optional, my friends and I hoisted our dinghy ashore on Necker Island in the British Virgin Islands. To our delight, goats ran freely, but the tiki bar that we found—a hidden gem off the beaten path—excited us more. It wasn't much more than a wooden shack that two brothers had pirated from a neighboring island. One of them flashed a machete, smiled, and went about chopping the fresh coconuts he had harvested moments earlier. He handed the carved coconuts to his brother, who filled them with rum and fresh lime juice. It was pure heaven. Sadly, Necker Island has become an exclusive resort, but it will always remain part of the inspiration for Lynn's Hula Hut and

Hula Hut Spirits, which is now bottled and sold online and in local bars and restaurants. I'm proud to share my story with you.

After years in the restaurant and design business in Colorado, I returned to Montauk, New York, to begin a new chapter. Montauk lies at the easternmost tip of Long Island and is known for its temperate climate and abundance of farms and vineyards. As you head east for the 120-mile drive from Manhattan, the hustle and bustle of the city gradually fades into a scenic stretch along a two-lane road that passes through the Hamptons, a series of small seaside hamlets. Farther east, quaint towns give way to long stretches of sandy beaches, summer resorts, and breathtaking glimpses of the Atlantic Ocean. My heart still flutters at the first sight of the sea. Most of us refer to Montauk as "the End." The Native Americans and early Dutch settlers called it "the promised land" on account of its rich soil and abundance of local seafood. I spent my childhood summers here with my loving mother and my father, a handsome, rugged lobsterman with a great sense of humor. As a tight-knit Italian and Spanish family, we shared our home with my grandparents, and my fondest childhood memories are of fishing and clamming with my father and helping Grandma Fiorita in her garden.

Returning to Montauk as an adult, I bought a long-bed pickup truck and converted it into a mobile tiki bar to cater private events throughout the Hamptons. It was my new calling, but it wasn't my first time slinging drinks here. A tavern owner had tried to reassure me—at the tender age of eighteen and with absolutely no training—"Don't worry, this is a beer and shot bar. It won't be busy. All the fishermen are out at sea." A nor'easter promptly blew in (just my luck), and the bar filled to the gills.

The money was great, but it was just a job then. When I came back, having my own bar gave me a purpose. It became my dream, and the challenges ahead felt exciting. I had my mobile tiki bar painted Sunset Orange Effect, a bona fide mid-century modern color. Large hibiscus flowers graced the sides, and my slogan—"Have tiki, will travel"—accentuated the door panels. A custom teak bar topped with a large thatched palapa covered the truck bed and provided an authentic island feel.

In 2012, Lynn's Hula Hut was finally open for business. Today, it is Montauk's tropical oasis, surrounded by large palms and adorned with bamboo and beach sand. A large Buddha greets you as you enter, and the smell of the sea intertwines with fresh basil and mint to transport you to paradise! It is also the birthplace of Hula Hut Spirits, which are used in a number of the cocktails in this book.

Here my love of design and mixology come together. It's also the place where I met my friend and coauthor, James O. Fraioli, a television producer and award-winning author of dozens of beautiful cookbooks, including one that garnered a coveted James Beard Award in 2014. We immediately bonded over our shared passions for great food, cocktails, and a fresh-is-best philosophy. Our fun, lighthearted book encourages you to escape, if only for an hour, to some faraway island brimming with sunshine, rum, and sparkling water. Let's toast to finding your own tropical paradise, wherever it may be, while you soak up the sun and get inspired to create your own tiki cocktails to enjoy with loved ones on that sandy beach someplace—even if it's in your own backyard.

TOOLS OF THE TRADE

Whether you're a professional mixologist or a backyard bartender, having the right bar tools is essential. I love to shop in thrift stores and hunt for vintage barware, like leather-bound ice buckets and unique glassware, for hosting parties. You can never have too many vintage tiki mugs, mid-century modern Collins glasses, or decanters. Attention-grabbing cocktail trays are a great way to serve your favorite concoctions—as is wearing a vintage cocktail apron. Beginners should start with a local restaurant or bar supply store. Here's what you need to get started.

BLENDER

A stick or immersion blender is fine for liquids, but always use a countertop model when blending ice, and *always* secure the lid before turning it on. It sounds like a basic step, but you'll be unpleasantly surprised if that lid is loose!

BOTTLES

Use decorative glass bottles fitted with pour spouts to store and serve your syrups.

CONTAINERS

For your purees, use plastic squeeze bottles, which you can find online or at restaurant supply stores—and buy them new. You don't want your tropical cocktails tasting sour!

CUTTING BOARD

Wood is good, but plastic works, too.

ICE BUCKET AND TONGS

An insulated bucket with a lid will keep your ice from melting on hot summer days.

JIGGER

Two-sided jiggers run the gamut of sizes. Invest in a good one that delineates a variety of fractions.

JUICER

Invest in a good-quality electric model. You're going to be juicing a lot of fruit, so it's worth the money.

KNIFE

I prefer one with a medium-size, nonserrated blade, such as a kitchen knife or chef's knife. Whatever kind you use, make sure it's sharp. A dull knife is more dangerous than a sharp one because it will slip more easily.

MUDDLER

This handheld rod with a flat, rounded bottom is used to extract herbal essences and crush fruits and other ingredients in the bottom of a glass. Again, wood is good, but plastic works, too.

PAPER PARASOLS

These are not strictly tools, but a must-have for that true island feel.

PEELER

A Y-shaped peeler gives you more control and cleaner twists, but in a pinch you can use the vegetable peeler that you already have in your kitchen drawer.

POUR SPOUT

Spring for the ones with built-in screens, which will keep fruit flies out of your syrups and spirits.

SHAKER

I prefer a cobbler shaker, which consists of three interlocking stainless-steel pieces: the cup, the strainer, and the cap. You can also use a mixing glass and a Hawthorne strainer (see Strainer).

SKEWERS

Short ones, about 4 inches, made of bamboo are great for garnishes.

STRAINER

If you make your drinks with a shaker that doesn't have a built-in strainer, make sure you either have a Hawthorne strainer on hand, which has a curved metal coil that allows you to adjust the level of the strain, or a julep strainer, which is bowl-shaped and slotted with small holes through which liquid can pass. There are a lot of cheap strainers on the market, most with loose springs that easily fall off. Look for a strainer that has some weight, doesn't feel flimsy, and has a nice tight and sturdy coil.

STRAWS

The more colorful, the better!

GLASSWARE & SERVING VESSELS

The glass, cup, or bowl in which you serve a drink is quite literally its foundation. Selecting one with the right size and shape is important. Each has its reason and purpose.

COCONUT SHELL

Making these from scratch will look great but takes a lot of time and effort. If you can't find them in a local store, it's better to buy them online.

COLLINS GLASS

A tall, cylindrical glass that holds between 8 and 14 ounces.

COUPE

Supposedly molded from Marie Antoinette's left breast, this old-fashioned Champagne glass now used for modern cocktails holds around 5 or 6 ounces. Chill in the freezer in advance.

FLUTE

With a tall, narrow bowl on a stem, this glass that holds between 4 and 6 ounces is the preferred serving vessel for sparkling wine.

HIGHBALL

Named for a railroad instrument that indicated speed, this is a cross between a Collins glass and a rocks glass, and holds 8 to 12 ounces.

HURRICANE GLASS

Resembling a glass-footed hurricane lantern, it can hold 12 to 20 ounces.

MARGARITA GLASS

An enlarged, modified coupe that can hold anywhere from 8 to 16 ounces.

MARTINI GLASS

A V-shaped glass with a long stem typically used to serve chilled and strained cocktails ranging from 6 to 12 ounces. Chill in the freezer in advance.

MASON JAR

A glass jar, with glass screw threads around the neck for a metal lid, that can hold 8 to 16 ounces.

PILSNER GLASS

A Collins glass with sass that tapers inward toward the bottom and holds between 8 and 12 ounces.

PINT GLASS

A 16-ounce glass either in an inverted conical shape or the nonik (pronounced "no-nick") variety, which swells outward toward the top.

ROCKS GLASS

A short, cylindrical glass that holds between 6 and 8 ounces. Large rocks glasses can hold up to 10 or 12 ounces.

SNIFTER

A short round bowl that has a narrow mouth and a glass foot; it can hold around 6 or 8 ounces.

TIKI BOWLS

Tiki bowls were and still are designed by tiki artists for those seeking a much larger ceramic vessel in which to serve more than 36 ounces of liquor for two or more people to share. The scorpion bowl is one such example. Other bowls—which often showcase artistic designs of Hawaiian and Polynesian villages, oceans, and gods emblazoned on the sides—can hold volumes over 52 ounces and satisfy the communal thirst of four or more adults. The volcano bowl is large enough to tackle this task and comes with a built-in crater in the center, into which goes a small pool of overproof rum, such as Bacardi 151, that you carefully can ignite to create volcanic ambience. There's nothing like sipping an oversize tropical libation through straws with friends amid a glowing flame!

TIKI MUGS

These artful ceramic drink vessels are a must-have when serving classic tiki cocktails. They come in a variety of colors, shapes, and sizes and are fun to use and display. Believed to be created at Don the Beachcomber, one of America's original tiki bars, tiki drinkware had its heyday in the 1960s and carried through the '80s and '90s when tiki and tropical-themed restaurants like Trader Vic's readily sold their mugs as souvenirs when they weren't filling them with tropical concoctions. Often depicting traditional Polynesian carvings and gods, the iconic tiki mug appeared in all sorts of styles from basic coconuts and pineapples to headhunters, spirits, skulls, hula girls, and rum barrels. You can find original vintage mugs today by scouring swap meets, garage sales, and websites such as eBay. Replicas and new tiki mugs are readily available online.

INGREDIENTS & GARNISHES

Selecting the proper base spirit for making your cocktails as well as infusing garnishes is important. Try not to resort to using cheap alcohol in either case. The quality of the liquor affects the quality of the flavor profile and the garnish and therefore the overall finished cocktail.

When experimenting with flavor-packed modifiers, such as bitters and syrups, always start with smaller amounts. Even those small amounts can alter the flavor profile of a drink quickly and drastically. You can always add more, but you can't take it out once you've poured it in.

Garnishes usually, though not exclusively, consist of slices, spears, twists, wedges, wheels, or whole pieces of fruit or sprigs, leaves, and sometimes blooms of herbs, edible flowers, and other tasty delights. Use your imagination, and remember that garnishes are meant to enhance the flavor of a cocktail and add visual appeal. Many cocktails can be served with one or more garnishes, while some are best left unadorned. If you decide to garnish, use fresh fruits and clean them thoroughly before use. Below you'll find some of the garnishes mentioned later in the book and directions on how to prepare them.

I often use the term "tiki couture" to refer to dressing or styling a cocktail. The right look sets the mood for a gathering, evokes a particular feeling or memory for your guests, and pleases the senses. Don't be afraid to get creative and tap in to the inspiration around you. You'd never put your cufflinks or earrings on before you picked out your outfit, so once you've made your drinks, use colorful straws, cocktail umbrellas, edible flowers, and other items to help you "accessorize" and put your signature on each cocktail you serve.

BERRIES

The fresher the berry, the better. Whether you use blackberries, blueberries, raspberries, or strawberries, always remove and discard the stems and leaves; then wash them thoroughly under cold running water before muddling, slicing, garnishing, or serving.

CHERRIES

When soaking cherries in liquor, keep in mind that they're quite dense and take significantly longer to infuse— approximately 2 to 3 weeks—than softer fruits like pineapple wedges (page 18), which take only 2 to 3 days.

CITRUS TWIST

Thoroughly rinse the fruit in warm water, and place it on its side on your cutting board. With a sharp knife, slice through the center of the fruit, exposing the flower-shaped center. Slice the halves into wheels ⅛ inch to ¼ inch wide, then slice through the rind and cut off the pulp to leave a long, thin strip of rind. Twist the rind into a coil.

If you have a channel knife (available at most kitchen or restaurant supply stores), you can do this quickly and easily, but be sure to cut the strip of rind off the fruit and twist it directly above the glass so that the flavorful oils from the zest spritz into your cocktail.

CITRUS WEDGE

Thoroughly rinse the fruit in warm water, and place it on its side on your cutting board. Using light pressure, roll the fruit on the board with your hand to soften the pulp inside. Then, with a sharp knife, slice off the ends of the fruit. Align your knife lengthwise on the fruit, and slice it in half. Turn each half flat side down, align your knife lengthwise again with the two cut ends, and slice in half. Turn each quarter flat side down, align your knife lengthwise one more time, and slice in half. Cover with a damp paper towel and refrigerate for up to 24 hours before serving.

CITRUS WHEEL

Thoroughly rinse the fruit in warm water, and place it on its side on your cutting board. With a sharp knife, slice off the ends of the fruit to expose the flower-shaped center. Align your knife lengthwise on the fruit, and slice halfway through, creating what will be the notch in each wheel that straddles the edge of the glass. Starting at one end, slice the fruit into wheels ⅛ inch to ¼ inch wide. Cover with a damp paper towel and refrigerate for up to 24 hours before serving.

CUCUMBER SPEAR

Thoroughly rinse the cucumber in warm water. You can leave the skin on or use a peeler to remove some of it to create stripes. Slice off the ends, align your knife lengthwise, and slice it in half. Turn each half flat side down, align your knife lengthwise, and slice in half again. Turn each quarter flat side down, align your knife lengthwise, and slice in half again. Place the spears in a shallow dish or tall glass, cover with water, and refrigerate for up to 24 hours before serving.

CUCUMBER WHEEL

Thoroughly rinse the cucumber in warm water. You can leave the skin on or use a peeler to remove some of it to create stripes. Slice off the ends and, starting at one end, slice the fruit into wheels ⅛ inch to ¼ inch wide. Lay each wheel flat, and make a slice from the center through one edge to create the notch that straddles the edge of the glass. Place in a bowl, cover with water, and refrigerate for up to 24 hours before serving.

BOUDREAUX'S BOURBON CHERRY BOMB

1 PINT CHERRIES, STEMS ON

2 CUPS MAKER'S MARK, BULLEIT, OR OTHER PREMIUM BOURBON

Fill a large mason jar with the cherries. Add the bourbon, secure the lid tightly, and store in a cool, dry place for 2 to 3 weeks. *Makes approximately 1 pint.*

TRAVERSE CITY CHERRY BOMB

A trip to Michigan inspired this recipe for rum-soaked cherries. I've never tasted more delicious cherries than the ones I had in Traverse City.

1 PINT CHERRIES, STEMS ON

1 CUP PREMIUM LIGHT RUM

1 CUP PREMIUM DARK RUM

Fill a large mason jar with the cherries, and add both rums. Secure the lid tightly, and turn the jar over several times to blend the rums. Let the cherries steep in a cool, dry place for 2 to 3 weeks. *Makes approximately 1 pint.*

One evening, a certain well-known country singer from Nashville showed up at Lynn's Hula Hut with his guitar. After most of our guests had gone home, he surprised us with a private concert. A couple of tunes and a couple of drinks later he loudly and proudly proclaimed himself a rough-and-tumble whiskey-drinkin' Southern boy with a high tolerance for bourbon and moonshine. So I offered him a Boudreaux's Bourbon Cherry Bomb, named after my crazy Cajun friend from southern Louisiana.

"Is that all you've got?" he hollered.

So I opened up the mason jar, pulled out a couple more cherries, and shouted back: "Open up, and come to mama!"

Four Cherry Bombs and several songs later, we called his driver and sent him off in true Montauk style.

EDIBLE FLOWERS

You can find edible flowers, such as orchids and hibiscus, at local farmers' markets when in season or online at specialty retailers, such as Gourmet SweetBotanicals.com or MarxFoods .com. Both sites ship overnight for maximum freshness. Rinse the flowers gently in cold water, and let them air-dry on a paper towel. Use them immediately, or store them in an airtight container in the refrigerator for up to 4 days. Make sure you order 100 percent edible flowers such as hibiscus, jasmine, lavender, lemon verbena, and nasturtiums. They'll make a beautiful statement when used as garnish.

HERBS

Basil, cilantro, mint, and rosemary all grow in an herb garden at the Hula Hut, and all make a wonderful addition to tropical cocktails. Always use fresh herbs, which are much more fragrant and add more depth to a drink than those expensive dried herbs in glass jars. Fresh herbs are relatively easy to grow outside in the summer or inside in a potted container near a windowsill in the winter. You'll find basil, cilantro, dill, lavender, mint, rosemary, sage, thyme, and more in the pages of this book. If you can't grow them yourself, you can always pick them up fresh at your local grocery store or farmers' market.

ICE

Size matters when it comes to ice. Use extra-large cubes in a rocks glass when serving premium liquors on the rocks, standard or medium-size cubes for drinks served in Collins or highball glasses, and crushed ice for most tropical concoctions. If you don't have a refrigerator that will make crushed ice for you, place the cubes in a sealable plastic freezer bag, and make sure the bag is completely sealed. Smash the cubes with a mallet, meat tenderizer, or other appropriate kitchen tool until the cubes break into small chips.

KIWI WHEEL

Thoroughly rinse the kiwi in warm water, and place it on its side on your cutting board. Slice off the ends of the fruit, and then slice it in half between the cut ends to expose the starburst center of the fruit. Slice the halves into wheels ⅛ inch to ¼ inch wide. If you prefer to use them skinless, trim the skin from around the wheels. (It's much easier than trying to peel the skin from the whole fruit while trying to hold on to it.) Lay each wheel flat and make a slice from the center through one edge of the wheel to create the notch that straddles the edge of the glass. Cover with a damp paper towel and refrigerate for up to 12 hours before serving.

JUICE

Always squeeze all your juices fresh. If I catch you with a store-bought plastic squeeze bottle of flavored water, I'll confiscate it!

LEMONS, LIMES, AND ORANGES

It's always a good idea to have a few fresh lemons, limes, and oranges readily available for spontaneous events or surprise guests. Citrus fruits release more juice when warm, so soak them in warm water for 10 to 15 minutes, or microwave them for 15 to 20 seconds on high, before use.

MANGOES

A healthy, ripe mango should be plump with a light green to reddish-yellow colored skin, depending on the variety. When you pick it up, it should feel heavier than it looks. It's ripe if the skin indents slightly when you squeeze it with your fingers, and it also should have a fruity fragrance. If only unripe mangoes are available, leave them on your kitchen counter (better if near sunlight or a window), and they'll ripen in a few days. If the mango has pronounced brown marks or feels mushy, it's too ripe.

MANGO SPEAR

Some grocery stores carry mango spears already prepared and ready to use. They're fresh, delicious, and a great time saver. If yours doesn't, here's how to make them.

Rinse the mango thoroughly in warm water, and stand it on its end on your cutting board. With a peeler or sharp paring knife, slice off the skin, working your way around the fruit. The mango is an oval-shaped fruit with a large, flat pit in the middle, so when holding it on its end, you'll see that it has two wide sides and two narrow sides. Slice down through the mango toward the center along one of the wide sides. If your knife hits the seed, move it slightly away from the center, and continue slicing. Cut as big a single piece as you can. Repeat on the other side, and slice off the fruit that remains on the two narrow sides. Cut the large pieces lengthwise into slices ½ inch to ¾ inch wide. Cover with a damp paper towel and refrigerate for up to 24 hours before serving. You can also place the spears in a tall jar, cover them with mango nectar, and store them in the fridge for up to 1 week.

MELONS

Melons are the sweet, fleshy fruit of a plant that originated in southwest Asia and Africa, and they reportedly were grown by European settlers in America as early as the 1600s. Many different varieties are widely available today, including cantaloupe, honeydew, and the summertime favorite, watermelon. They all make a delicious garnish.

CANTALOUPE OR HONEYDEW WEDGE

Thoroughly rinse the melon in warm water, and place it on its side on your cutting board. Slice it in half from one end to the other. Using a spoon, scrape the seeds from the center of the fruit and discard them. Lay each half flat side down, and slice in half from end to end again. Place each quarter rind side down, and slice in half from end to end one more time. Slice each piece into 2-inch wedges by cutting through the flesh and just into the rind, making sure not to cut all the way through. Separate the wedges from the rind by slicing between the fruit and the rind from end to end. Cover with a damp paper towel and refrigerate for up to 24 hours before serving.

WATERMELON WEDGE

Thoroughly rinse a seedless watermelon in warm water, and place it on its side on your cutting board. Slice it in half from end to end. Lay each half flat side down, and slice in half from end to end again. Place each quarter rind side down, and slice in half from end to end one more time. Slice each piece into wedges 1 to 2 inches wide by cutting through the flesh and just into the rind, making sure not to cut all the way through. Separate the wedges from the rind by slicing between the fruit and the rind from end to end. Cover with a damp paper towel and refrigerate for up to 24 hours before serving.

MELON BALLS

Thoroughly rinse your melon of choice in warm water, and place it on its side on your cutting board. Slice it in half from end to end. For cantaloupe, honeydew, and other varieties with seeds in the center, use a spoon to scrape out the seeds and discard them. With a melon baller or small ice cream scoop, scoop out the flesh until only the rind remains. Cover with a damp paper towel and refrigerate for up to 24 hours before serving.

PINEAPPLES

Despite its origin in parts of inland Central America, the pineapple is considered one of the most Polynesian of tropical fruits. Over time, this excellent fruit has served as a staple of native feasts and trade with Europeans and as a universal symbol of celebration and hospitality. If you look carefully, you'll see the symbol used in architecture and design on banisters, door knockers, and elsewhere. Any tiki-themed event or gathering should feature a few symbolic pineapples to welcome guests and set the mood.

This delicious fruit explodes with sweet, juicy flavor when eaten, and it is an excellent source of antioxidants, vitamins (A, B complex, and C), and minerals. Per serving, it has roughly the same number of calories as an apple, and it makes a colorful, versatile garnish or appetizer for any event.

After a pineapple is picked, it doesn't continue to ripen, as many other fleshy fruits do. Here are four tips to help you pick a fresh, sweet, and juicy pineapple every time.

1. A ripe pineapple will have well-developed and relatively flat eyes—the spiked, rough circles making up the geometric pattern on the rind.
2. A fresh pineapple has healthy green leaves and golden-yellow skin. Some light green coloring near the stem is okay. If the leaves are more brown than green or if the skin is reddish-brown, wrinkled, cracked, or moldy, keep looking.
3. The juicier the pineapple, the heavier it will feel. A ripe one will feel firm but give slightly beneath your fingers when you squeeze it. Also try plucking a leaf from the top to check for ripeness. If it comes out with no resistance, the pineapple may be rotten.
4. Ripe pineapples have a sweet scent. If the fruit has no scent, it's not ripe. If it smells of vinegar or alcohol, then it's overripe.

PINEAPPLE WEDGE

For my garnishes, I prefer to leave the skin and core, which requires less prep and looks more organic.

Rinse the pineapple thoroughly in warm water and place it on its side on your cutting board. Slice off the base and the leaves. (If you want to remove the skin, set the pineapple on its base, and slice off the skin, sawing downward and working your way around the fruit.) To remove any remaining eyes, cut a V-shaped groove diagonally down each row, again working your way around the fruit. Lay the pineapple on its side, align your knife lengthwise, and cut it in half. Place each half flat side down, align your knife lengthwise again, and cut it into quarters. Stand each quarter up, and slice downward to remove the woody core (optional). Lay each quarter on its side, and slice crosswise into wedges ½ to ¾ inch wide. Make a 1-inch cut through the "core point" of each wedge. Cover with a damp paper towel and refrigerate for up to 48 hours before serving.

DRUNKEN PINEAPPLE WEDGES

This is my favorite garnish, which I also serve hot off the grill to get the party started. It's great on skewers with coconut curried shrimp or chicken.

1 PINEAPPLE

2 CUPS HULA HUT HULA JUICE SPICED COCONUT RUM

2 TABLESPOONS FRESHLY GROUND CINNAMON

Wash the pineapple thoroughly and cut it into ½-inch-thick wedges, leaving the skin on. Fill a large mason jar with the wedges, pour in both rums, and add the cinnamon. Secure the lid tightly and turn the jar over several times to blend the rums and spice. Let the pineapple steep in a cool, dry place for 2 to 3 days.

RUM

Ah, yes, that distilled tropical beverage made from sweet sugarcane and molasses. It's been the go-to spirit for pirates, buccaneers, and the navies of various empires that once sailed through the Caribbean. It's also one of the most frequently featured liquors in tiki cocktails.

Today, many countries around the globe, including the United States, produce rum, although rum connoisseurs proclaim that the best rums still come from the Caribbean and the southern hemisphere, where the majority of the world's rum production still takes place. Rum is available in different grades, from light to gold to dark, all used in cocktail making. More expensive premium rums typically are reserved for sipping neat or over ice. As with any high-priced, top-shelf liquor, you shouldn't mix a fine artisanal rum; that's what the less expensive rums are for.

Some rums are spiced (such as Sailor Jerry), flavored, or overproof (like Bacardi 151). Note that when substituting these "altered" rums in a cocktail recipe, you'll change the flavor profile of the drink—for better . . . or for worse! For recipes that simply call for "rum," stick to a traditional rum, and reserve rum variations for recipes that specify when to use a spiced, flavored, or overproof rum.

SYRUPS

Syrups don't just add sweetness to a cocktail. They can balance bitter or acidic drinks and enhance flavor profiles in a variety of subtle but important ways. It truly is simple: heat equal parts sugar and water until the sugar dissolves. Easier yet, if your home's boiler or water heater is strong enough, pour the hot water and sugar directly into a jar, secure the lid, and shake vigorously until the sugar dissolves. If you prefer, you can use honey, brown sugar, or agave nectar instead. But keep in mind that honey or brown sugar will give the cocktail an amber hue.

Infusing flavor into syrup is just as easy, and you can use almost any fruits, herbs, or spices. Fresh basil, cilantro, mint, and rosemary—as in the Rosemary Lemon Syrup on page 22—are among my favorites. Try infusing syrup with lavender (below). It will transform an average martini into an elegant cocktail. Experiment with spices in syrups, such as cardamom, cinnamon, clove, and curry. Just a tiny amount of syrup made with any of those spices can take the flavor profile of your cocktail to the next level.

You can also substitute herbal tea for water when making simple syrup. I like to use chamomile, jasmine, or orange-ginger tea. They're delicious and convenient if you're in a hurry. Don't be afraid to raid your cabinet and refrigerator and have some fun!

LAVENDER LEMON SYRUP

The fragrance of lavender and lemon add an undeniable sophistication to any cocktail.

2 CUPS WATER

¼ CUP EDIBLE LAVENDER FLOWERS

1½ CUPS RAW SUGAR, OR ½ CUP AGAVE NECTAR

1 TABLESPOON FRESH LEMON JUICE

In a medium saucepan, bring the water and lavender to a boil. Add the sugar and stir until it dissolves. Add the lemon juice, lower the heat, cover, and simmer for 3 to 5 minutes. Remove from the heat and set aside to cool to room temperature. Strain through a fine-mesh strainer into a bottle, and refrigerate. (The cooled syrup will keep in the refrigerator for up to 1 week.) *Makes 3 cups.*

Try it in the Lavender Lemon Tikitini (page 100) or the Lavender Coconut Cocktail (page 119).

LIGHT SIMPLE SYRUP

This is a healthier alternative to traditional simple syrups made from refined sugar.

2 CUPS WATER

½ CUP AGAVE NECTAR

In a medium saucepan, bring the water to a boil over high heat. Whisk in the agave nectar. Remove from the heat and continue whisking until thoroughly blended. Cover and set aside to cool to room temperature. Pour into a bottle and refrigerate. (The cooled syrup will keep in the refrigerator for up to 1 week.) *Makes 2½ cups.*

Use it in the Cucumber Sorbet Saketini (page 161) or the Island Fashioned (page 157).

ROSEMARY LEMON SYRUP

The aroma of fresh rosemary and lemon is extremely calming. It will relax you even before the first sip.

2 CUPS WATER

3 OR 4 SPRIGS ROSEMARY, ABOUT 3 INCHES LONG

1½ CUPS RAW SUGAR, OR ½ CUP AGAVE NECTAR

1 TABLESPOON FRESH LEMON JUICE

In a medium saucepan, combine the water and rosemary and bring to a boil over high heat. Add the sugar and stir until it dissolves. Add the lemon juice, reduce the heat to maintain a simmer, cover, and cook for 3 to 5 minutes. Remove from the heat and set aside to cool to room temperature. Strain through a fine-mesh strainer into a bottle and refrigerate. (The syrup will keep in the refrigerator for up to 1 week.) *Makes 3 cups.*

Try this syrup in the Rosemary Lemonade (page 86).

PUREES

To create these purees, you'll need a blender, food processor, or high-speed blender like a NutriBullet, the last of which is my weapon of choice because it produces a perfectly even and smooth puree in seconds. Use the freshest ingredients available, particularly fruits and vegetables. I shop the Montauk Farmers Market every summer Thursday for fresh, local produce grown in the area's rich soil. Be sure to rinse all your produce thoroughly before using.

As you'll see in the recipes that follow, I add citrus juice, water, or lemonade to give my purees a smooth texture, along with a bit of agave nectar to balance the flavors and add some sweetness. When using jalapeños, as in the Hot Basil & Berry Puree (page 25) and the Cucumber, Cilantro & Jalapeño Puree (see below), include the seeds for extra heat if you like more kick. When storing a puree in a plastic squeeze bottle, make sure that the bottle has a dispenser tip large enough for the mixture to flow freely.

Not only will these purees enhance your cocktails, but they're amazing when used in ceviche, added to other seafood dishes, or drizzled on salads. You can puree just about any kind of fruit, vegetable, or fresh herb. Visit your local farmers' market for inspiration.

CUCUMBER, CILANTRO & JALAPEÑO PUREE

The beauty of this spicy, cool, refreshing puree lies in its versatility. Use it for a punch of flavor in cocktails, or incorporate it into ceviche or Thai chicken salad and lettuce wraps. Keep a bottle in your fridge and get creative.

8 MEDIUM CUCUMBERS

2 TO 3 JALAPEÑOS

1 LARGE BUNCH CILANTRO

4 TO 6 TABLESPOONS LYNN'S LEMONADE (PAGE 32)

Thoroughly rinse the cucumbers, jalapeños, and cilantro. Cut the cucumbers in half lengthwise, leaving the skin on for crunch and color. Cut them into 1-inch chunks and set aside.

Cut the jalapeños in half lengthwise. Slice each half into smaller chunks, up to ¼ inch wide. Leave the seeds in for extra heat if desired.

Remove and discard the stems from the cilantro bunch and coarsely chop the leaves.

Combine the cucumber, jalapeños, and cilantro in a food processor or blender. Add the lemonade and puree. The mixture should be slightly pulpy. Transfer to a plastic squeeze bottle and store in the refrigerator for up to 3 days. *Makes 3 to 4 cups.*

FENNEL ORANGE PUREE

This unexpected but delicious blend is perfect during the summer months. Use it in cocktails and on garden salads and fresh seafood.

½ CUP CHOPPED FRESH FENNEL

1 MEDIUM BLOOD ORANGE, OR 2 MANDARIN ORANGES, PEELED

2 TABLESPOONS AGAVE NECTAR

¼ CUP WATER

Combine the fennel, orange, agave nectar, and water in a food processor or blender, and puree until smooth. Transfer to a plastic squeeze bottle and store in the refrigerator for up to 3 days. *Makes 2 cups.*

HOT BASIL & BERRY PUREE

This tropical concoction is great in cocktails, of course, but it's also amazing over lemon sorbet as a dessert.

¾ CUP STRAWBERRIES

½ CUP BLUEBERRIES

8 TO 10 LARGE BASIL LEAVES

½ JALAPEÑO (USE MORE OR LESS DEPENDING ON DESIRED HEAT)

¼ CUP AGAVE NECTAR

¼ CUP LYNN'S LEMONADE (PAGE 32)

Rinse the strawberries, blueberries, basil, and jalapeño thoroughly. Remove the stems from the strawberries and jalapeño. Slice the jalapeño in half lengthwise, leaving the seeds for extra heat, if desired. In a food processor or blender, combine the strawberries, blueberries, basil, jalapeño, agave nectar, and lemonade and puree until smooth. Transfer to a plastic squeeze bottle and store in the refrigerator for up to 3 days. *Makes 2 cups.*

Use this in the Hot Basil & Berry Lemonade (page 65).

HOT MANGO PUREE

This absolutely excellent puree is delicious in tiki drinks as well as on seafood.

1 JALAPEÑO

2 CUPS DICED MANGO

1 TABLESPOON SRIRACHA

3 TABLESPOONS FRESH LIME JUICE

3 TABLESPOONS WATER

3 TABLESPOONS AGAVE NECTAR

Rinse the jalapeño thoroughly and remove the stem. Slice the jalapeño lengthwise and then across, cutting each piece in half. In a food processor or blender, combine the jalapeño pieces, mango, sriracha, lime juice, water, and agave nectar and puree. Transfer to a plastic squeeze bottle and refrigerate for up to 3 days. *Makes 2½ cups.*

Add this to the Hot Mango Mamacita (page 67) and *¡ay caramba!*

MANGO & MINT PUREE

This puree goes into many of my drinks, and it also works well on salads and seafood. You can turn it into a salad dressing by adding fresh lemon juice and olive oil. Don't be afraid to experiment!

2 CUPS DICED MANGO

⅔ CUP CHOPPED FRESH MINT

2 TABLESPOONS AGAVE NECTAR

2 TABLESPOONS LYNN'S LEMONADE (PAGE 32)

Combine the mango, mint, agave nectar, and lemonade in a food processor or blender and puree until smooth. Transfer to a plastic squeeze bottle and store in the refrigerator for up to 2 days. *Makes 2 cups.*

Use this to make the Mango, Mint & Rum Spritzer (page 75).

SMOKED PINEAPPLE & SAGE PUREE

You'll love the surprisingly delicious smoky sweetness of this puree, which can double as a marinade for chicken.

2 CUPS PINEAPPLE CHUNKS

2 TABLESPOONS AGAVE NECTAR

¼ CUP CHOPPED FRESH SAGE

1 TEASPOON SMOKED HOT PAPRIKA, OR TO TASTE

1 TABLESPOON LYNN'S LEMONADE (PAGE 32)

Combine the pineapple, agave nectar, sage, paprika, and lemonade in a food processor or blender and puree until smooth. Transfer to a plastic squeeze bottle and store in the refrigerator for up to 2 days. *Makes 2½ cups.*

Add this to the Tahitian Snake Charmer (page 80).

WATERMELON & BASIL PUREE

This fresh and delectable puree offers a sweet, refreshing taste of summer that can be used as a dressing on a fresh tomato and mozzarella salad or on chilled shrimp as an alternative to cocktail sauce. Get creative with it!

1 SMALL SEEDLESS WATERMELON

⅔ CUP CHOPPED FRESH BASIL

¼ CUP AGAVE NECTAR

Cut the watermelon in half and trim off the bitter rind. Slice the melon flesh into 2-inch cubes.

Combine the watermelon, basil, and agave nectar in a food processor or blender and puree until smooth. Transfer to a plastic squeeze bottle and store in the refrigerator for up to 3 days. *Makes 3 to 4 cups.*

This puree adds a hint of fresh herbiness to the Montauk Marine Cooler (page 81).

INFUSIONS

What I love most about infusing liquors is the creativity that it allows. Italians have been infusing and spiking acqua di limone or limonata for generations. Grandmother Fiorita added her fresh limonata and two ice cubes to my grandfather's homemade wine during the hot summer months, garnishing it with fresh basil, thyme, peaches, and plums. She also soaked her homegrown figs and peaches in the red wine that my grandfather made. Pears infused in homemade grappa always made our family gatherings interesting.

To begin, you'll need a 2- to 3-gallon glass jar; these are available in a variety of shapes and styles. When using a jar with a spigot, always check for leaks before filling it with a costly, premium liquor. Fill the jar with water and place a paper towel under the spigot to see if it leaks. Also choose a jar with an airtight lid. Infusion times vary, depending on the ingredients. Pineapples, melons, and berries don't need as much time as dense-skinned cherries. Taste test your creation after a week to check the level of flavor. When using hot peppers, you may want to test it after just 2 or 3 days, at which point you can remove the peppers so your infusion doesn't get too spicy

Because of its neutral flavor, vodka is the most versatile spirit to infuse. But don't stop there. Bourbons, rums, and tequilas are also delicious when infused with fresh fruits, herbs, spices, and even vegetables such as hot peppers and onions. Gin itself is an infusion, but you can always add to it. The possibilities are endless, so create your own signature infusions with the freshest ingredients for the best results. Then marvel at the bevy of different cocktails that you can make from just one jar and a variety of mixers.

An important note: You may want to sample the fruit as your infusion runs low, but don't. The fruit filters impurities in the liquor and will taste bad. Discard or compost it, and slice some fresh fruit to start a new batch.

APPLE CINNAMON BOURBON

This infusion is as American as apple pie. Its smooth apple and cinnamon flavor and aroma are comfort in a jar. You can use it in festive autumn cocktails, serve it warm at holiday celebrations, or pour it over ice with lemonade and fresh mint or fruit during spring and summer. You'll love the versatility of this four-season blend.

10 TO 12 HONEYCRISP OR GALA APPLES

4 TO 6 CINNAMON STICKS

2 LITERS JACK DANIEL'S, MAKER'S MARK, OR OTHER PREMIUM BOURBON

Rinse the apples thoroughly and remove the stems. Cut the apples into quarters and place in a 2- to 3-gallon glass jar. Add the cinnamon sticks and bourbon and close the lid tightly. Let stand on the counter, out of direct sunlight, for at least 2 weeks, stirring daily. Taste it at the end of the first week and, if you prefer a milder spice profile, remove the cinnamon. *Makes about 2 liters.*

CARIBBEAN COMFORT INFUSION

Cinnamon is commonly used in many Caribbean cocktails and local cuisine like Jamaican jerk chicken. The essence of cinnamon is said to have a calming effect. Some cultures believe cinnamon is an aphrodisiac. I always connect cinnamon to comfort, which is why I call this infusion Caribbean Comfort.

1 PINEAPPLE

2 CINNAMON STICKS, ABOUT 4 INCHES LONG

2 (750 ML) BOTTLES HULA HUT HULA JUICE SPICED COCONUT RUM

1 LITER CHINOLA PASSION FRUIT LIQUEUR

Rinse the pineapple thoroughly, lay it on its side, and slice off the top and bottom. Stand the pineapple upright and cut the skin off in strips, starting at the top. Lay the remaining cylinder of pineapple flesh on its side and cut it into 1- to 2 inch slices. Quarter the slices and place them in a 2- to 3-gallon glass jar. Add the cinnamon sticks, rum, and liqueur and seal the jar tightly. Let stand on the counter, out of direct sunlight, for at least 1 week. Stir daily. *Makes about 2.5 liters.*

This blend makes an appearance in the Toasted Coconut (page 133) and the Caribbean Comfort Cocktail (page 125).

COCO LOCO INFUSION

This perfectly balanced and versatile infusion is great when chilled and served straight up in a martini glass or on the rocks.

1 PINEAPPLE

1.25 LITERS MILAGRO SILVER OR OTHER PREMIUM SILVER TEQUILA

750 ML COCONUT RUM

Rinse the pineapple thoroughly, lay it on its side, and slice off the top and bottom. Stand the pineapple upright and cut the skin off in strips, starting at the top. Lay the remaining cylinder of pineapple flesh on its side and cut it into 1- to 2-inch slices. Quarter the slices and place them in a 2- to 3-gallon glass jar. Add the tequila and rum and seal the jar tightly. Let stand on the counter, out of direct sunlight, for at least 1 week, stirring daily. *Makes approximately 2 liters.*

This infusion appears in many of the cocktails in this book, including the Brazilian Breezer (page 111) and the Mayan Sunrise (page 77).

CUCUMBER CHILE VODKA

The coolness of the cucumber in this infusion tames the heat of the pepper and results in a unique, well-balanced flavor.

6 CUCUMBERS

2 THAI CHILE PEPPERS, OR 3 OR 4 JALAPEÑOS

2 LITERS PREMIUM VODKA

Rinse the cucumbers and peppers thoroughly. Leaving the skin on, cut the cucumbers into ½-inch slices, and place in a 2- to 3-gallon glass jar. Slice one of the peppers lengthwise to expose the seeds, which will release the heat, then place both peppers in the jar. Pour the vodka into the jar and close the lid tightly. Let stand on the counter, out of direct sunlight, for at least 1 week. Stir daily. *Makes about 2 liters.*

> **NOTE:** Thai chiles sometimes can prove difficult to find and can be too hot for some, but three or four jalapeños would be a good substitute. Several of my signature cocktails use this infusion, including the Hot Pink Drink (page 69) the Hot Cucumber Tikitini (page 99), and various Bloody Marys.

CUCUMBER VODKA

This is one of the most versatile infusions that you can make. It pairs well with fresh herbs, such as basil, cilantro, and mint, and serves as the base for an extremely smooth and refreshing cocktail each and every time.

4 TO 6 LARGE CUCUMBERS

2 LITERS PREMIUM VODKA

Rinse the cucumbers thoroughly. Cut off the ends and discard. Cut the cucumbers into ¼-inch slices and place them into a 2- to 3-gallon glass jar. Add the vodka, secure the lid, and store on the counter, out of direct sunlight, for 1 to 2 weeks. Stir daily. Strain through a fine-mesh sieve, then store in the refrigerator in a sealed glass container. *Makes about 2 liters.*

SMOKED PINEAPPLE INFUSION

You can also enjoy this infusion on the rocks or chilled and served up in a martini glass.

1 PINEAPPLE

1 (750 ML) BOTTLE DOS HOMBRES MEZCAL

1 (750 ML) BOTTLE HULA HUT LÉ TAHITIAN VANILLA & PINEAPPLE VODKA

Rinse the pineapple thoroughly, lay it on its side, and slice off the top and bottom. Stand the pineapple upright and cut the skin off in strips, starting from the top. Lay the remaining cylinder of pineapple flesh on its side and cut it into 1- to 2-inch-thick slices. Quarter the slices and place them in a 2- to 3-gallon glass jar. Add the mezcal and vodka, then seal the jar tightly. Let stand on the counter, out of direct sunlight, for at least 1 week. Stir daily. *Makes about 1.5 liters.*

LYNN'S LEMONADE

This is a healthy and delicious substitute for sweet and sour mix, traditional powdered lemonades, or juices made from frozen concentrate, all of which are oversweet and loaded with sugar. Agave nectar is a natural sweetener derived from the same plant used to make tequila. In Mexico, the plant is called aguamiel, or honey water. The Aztecs believed that it came from the gods, and they used the liquid from its core to flavor foods and drinks. Many health-conscious consumers prefer it as their sweetener of choice.

1 GALLON NONCARBONATED SPRING WATER, WARMED SLIGHTLY

½ TO 1 CUP AGAVE NECTAR (TO TASTE)

6 LEMONS

Pour the water into a large glass pitcher, making sure to leave enough room for the agave nectar and lemons. The warmth of the water helps the agave nectar to dissolve thoroughly. You can also place the pitcher in a sunny spot for an hour or so to get the water to the right temperature for blending the ingredients. Add the agave nectar to taste, and stir until it dissolves.

Roll the lemons on a hard surface to release the juice from the fruit pulp. Slice them in half and juice the lemon halves into a bowl, using a mini strainer or citrus press to catch the seeds. Add the juice to the pitcher and stir well. Chill before serving. *Makes 1 gallon.*

Because it doesn't overpower but subtly complements other natural flavors, you'll find this lemonade in many of my recipes, including April Showers (page 41), Mandarin & Fennel Iced Tea (page 73), and Tahitian Snake Charmer (page 80).

PINEAPPLE JALAPEÑO VODKA

The combination of spicy and sweet is a very pleasant surprise in this infusion, as the pineapple balances the heat wonderfully. In fact, this infusion is amazing just on its own over ice. Feel free to get creative, as there's really no wrong way to enjoy this cocktail.

1 PINEAPPLE

4 TO 6 LARGE JALAPEÑOS (TO TASTE)

2 LITERS PREMIUM VODKA

Rinse the pineapple thoroughly. Slice off the top and bottom. Stand the pineapple upright and cut the skin off the sides in strips. Lay the remaining cylinder of pineapple flesh on its side and cut it into 1- to 2-inch slices, then place them in a 2- to 3-gallon glass jar. Slice the peppers in half lengthwise and place them in the jar. Add the vodka and close the lid tightly. Let stand on the counter, out of direct sunlight, for at least 1 week. Stir daily. *Makes about 2 liters.*

This infusion appears in several Hula Hut cocktails, including the Mayan Chocolate (page 76).

PINEAPPLE VANILLA VODKA

This infusion calms the senses and is simply amazing on its own over ice.

1 PINEAPPLE

1 TAHITIAN VANILLA BEAN (4 TO 6 INCHES LONG)

3 (750 ML) BOTTLES HULA HUT LÉ TAHITIAN VANILLA & PINEAPPLE VODKA

Rinse the pineapple thoroughly, lay it on its side, and slice off the top and bottom. Stand the pineapple upright and cut the skin off in strips, starting at the top. Lay the remaining cylinder of pineapple flesh on its side and cut it into 1- to 2-inch slices. Quarter the slices and place them in a 2- to 3-gallon glass jar. Score the vanilla bean lengthwise to release the flavor. Place the vanilla bean in the jar, add the vodka, and seal tightly. Let stand on the counter, out of direct sunlight, for at least 1 week, stirring daily. *Makes about 2 liters.*

This sweet and earthy infusion goes into many of my cocktails, such as the Tahitian Lemon Drop (page 103) and Mellow Yellow (page 79).

PINK LEMONADE

Pomegranates are an exception to my fresh-juicing rule. Separating the seeds from the rind and then the juice from the seeds should qualify as an Olympic event. Better to buy pomegranate juice, but make sure that it's 100 percent pure pomegranate juice. I like the Pom brand, which most grocery stores carry.

1 GALLON NONCARBONATED WARM SPRING WATER

1 CUP UNSWEETENED POMEGRANATE JUICE

½ TO 1 CUP AGAVE NECTAR (TO TASTE)

6 LEMONS

Pour the water into a large glass pitcher, making sure to leave enough room for the other ingredients. The water should be slightly warm. The warm water helps the agave nectar dissolve thoroughly. You can also place the pitcher of water in a sunny spot for an hour or so to get the water to the right temperature for blending the ingredients. Add the pomegranate juice and agave nectar to taste, and stir until the nectar dissolves.

Roll the lemons on a hard surface to release the juice from the fruit pulp. Slice them in half and juice the lemon halves into a bowl, using a mini strainer or citrus press to catch the seeds. Add the juice to the pom mixture and stir well. Chill before serving. *Makes about 1 gallon.*

TAHITIAN BLEND INFUSION

I use this blend year-round in practically everything, especially eggnog and warm cider during the holidays.

1 (4-INCH) KNOB FRESH GINGER

2 LITERS AGED RUM

3 TAHITIAN VANILLA BEANS, SPLIT LENGTHWISE

4 WHOLE CLOVES

2 OR 3 CINNAMON STICKS (ABOUT 4 INCHES LONG)

½ TEASPOON FRESHLY GRATED NUTMEG

ZEST OF 1 MANDARIN ORANGE (AVOID THE BITTER WHITE PITH)

2 HONEYCRISP APPLES

Peel the ginger, cut it into ⅛-inch slices, and place the slices in the bottom of a 2- to 3-gallon glass jar. Add the rum, vanilla beans, cloves, cinnamon sticks, nutmeg, orange zest, and apples. Secure the lid and store on the counter, out of direct sunlight, for 1 to 2 weeks before serving. *Makes about 2 liters.*

TECHNIQUES

Before you begin making cocktails, have all your tools at hand and ingredients prepared. A good rule of thumb: always smile and never let 'em see you sweat! I prep pitchers of cocktails ahead of time and store them in the refrigerator for up to 2 days before serving. Batching drinks—the industry term—allows you to get more creative in the moment, but remember to write down measurements and ingredients as you go. Trust me, you won't remember if you taste test along the way . . . and you must straw-taste your creations before you serve them.

BLEND

When using an immersion blender, keep the blades well below the surface of the liquid. You don't want to wind up wearing your cocktail. When making frozen drinks, pulse in a blender in short bursts to break up the ice without breaking the motor.

CHILL

If you don't have time to chill your martini glasses thoroughly in the freezer before making your drink, fill the glasses with icewater while you make the drink.

MUDDLE

When muddling herbs and other flora, press firmly to extract the plants' essences and oils—but don't mash them. Press harder to crush fruit.

RIM

When rimming a cocktail glass, start by squeezing the garnish or one of the garnishes (lemon, lime, jalapeño, or pineapple, for example) around the outside edge of the glass; then roll the outside edge in the salt, sugar, or other rimming mixture. That way the mixture won't blend into the drink and change the way it's supposed to taste.

SHAKE

Do it like bartenders do: horizontally over the shoulder. But make sure the cap's on tight. You want to shake your drink—not hurl it behind you!

HULA HUT COCKTAILS

My passion for tropical cocktails began when a friend and I rode a motorcycle around Mexico's Riviera Maya from Mérida to the country of Belize. It was still rural then, with few stops other than the occasional tiki bar on a remote beach. The drinks were simple and had few ingredients—just fresh fruits and juices mixed with tequila or rum. But they were absolutely delicious and much more refreshing than the sugary concoctions served stateside. Call it love in a coconut cup. That experience and many like it changed the way I make drinks, providing the inspiration for what are now my signature cocktails at Lynn's Hula Hut.

Many of these cocktails intentionally consist of ingredients that I can source locally. Whether in Montauk or abroad, I always search for the nearest farm stand or fruit tree. There's nothing better than stumbling upon those small, out-of-the-way places to eat and drink and venturing through an overgrown tropical path to find sugar-white sand caressed by a translucent, aquamarine sea. These cocktails will help you capture the feeling of that same experience wherever you may be.

APRIL SHOWERS

SERVES 1

Lemon verbena is prized for its intoxicating citrus aroma. This drink's winning combination of bracing cucumber, sweet elderflower liqueur, and the scent of lemon verbena provides a calming sensation from the first sip. It's as refreshing as warm sunshine after a cool spring shower.

4 CUCUMBER SLICES

½ OUNCE ST-GERMAIN OR OTHER ELDERFLOWER LIQUEUR

1½ OUNCES CUCUMBER VODKA (PAGE 32)

LYNN'S LEMONADE (PAGE 32)

1 SPRIG LEMON VERBENA, FOR GARNISH

In a Collins glass, combine 3 of the cucumber slices and the St-Germain and muddle. Fill the glass with ice and add the vodka. Top with some lemonade, then pour the contents of the glass into a cocktail shaker. Shake vigorously for 5 seconds. Return the cocktail to the glass, garnish with the lemon verbena sprig and the remaining cucumber slice, and serve with a straw.

BLUE BAYOU LEMONADE

SERVES 1

Louisiana is a melting pot of Spanish, West African, French, Native American, and Caribbean cultures. French Caribbean culture made a significant mark on New Orleans beginning in the early 1880s, when there was a mass exodus from Haiti to NOLA following the Haitian Revolution. As a result, Creole culture made an indelible mark on Louisiana. Many more emigrants from St. Barts and St. Maarten settled in Louisiana, establishing a thriving community and incorporating additional aspects of Caribbean architecture, food, and music into Louisiana's culture. Cajun and Caribbean colonies also sprang up along the many bayous where fish, game, and fruits were plentiful. This cocktail is a staple at my friend Luke's fishing camps in southwestern Louisiana.

¼ CUP BLUEBERRIES

½ OUNCE AGAVE NECTAR

2½ OUNCES PREMIUM BOURBON

6 OUNCES LYNN'S LEMONADE (PAGE 32)

1 LEMON TWIST, FOR GARNISH

Rinse the berries thoroughly and place them in a 12-ounce mason jar. Add the agave nectar and muddle well. Add the bourbon, fill the jar with ice, and top with the lemonade. Garnish with the lemon twist and enjoy, y'all!

NOTE: You can substitute wild berries found along the bayous in Louisiana for the blueberries.

BOUDREAUX'S BAYOU BERRY TEA

SERVES 1

My wild and crazy Cajun buddy Boudreaux kidnapped me and a friend from the Maple Leaf Bar in the Leonidas neighborhood of New Orleans many moons ago. He drove us to the swamp for a *fais do-do*—a Cajun dance celebration—at his brother's fishing camp. For three fun-filled days and nights, we feasted on alligator boudin, crawfish, and muscadine moonshine. This is my version of Boudreaux's hard-hitting berry moonshine, smooth but not quite as hard.

4 MUSCADINE BERRIES (SEE NOTE), PLUS EXTRA FOR GARNISH

JUICE OF ½ LEMON

2½ OUNCES MAKER'S MARK OR OTHER PREMIUM BOURBON

1 OUNCE AGAVE NECTAR

SASSAFRAS TEA (SEE NOTE)

1 SUGARCANE STALK (SEE NOTE), FOR GARNISH

1 ORANGE SECTION, FOR GARNISH

Cut the berries in half and muddle them with the lemon juice in a 16-ounce mason jar. Add the bourbon and agave nectar, and fill the jar with ice. Add the tea to within 1 to 2 inches from the top. Secure the lid on the jar and shake for a few seconds. Remove the lid and stir the drink with the sugarcane stalk, leaving it in for presentation. Garnish with additional berries and an orange section.

> **NOTE:** Muscadine berries are large, dark purple, and about the size of a grape. They grow wild in southern Louisiana and teem with antioxidants. If needed, you can use blackberries for the muscadines, and black or green tea for the sassafras.

BOURBON BASH

Names have been withheld to protect the not so innocent, but the Boys on the Bus, as I call them, inspired this cocktail. A few years ago, a bunch of southern guys drove up from the Carolinas for their annual trip to participate in one of several fishing tournaments held in Montauk Harbor. Their touring bus dropped anchor for several days in a parking lot near the Hula Hut, which hadn't opened yet. They sat and watched as I shoveled sand, planted palms, and readied the bar for the season. Introducing themselves, they said, "You need a break. Try this." I took a swig from the mason jar they handed me. Deliciously smooth. I chugged some more, and one of them said, "Whoa, simmer down now, girl. That's moonshine." Before long, their lightning in a bottle sent me to my hammock for a nice, long nap, but it also prompted this delicious drink. Thanks, guys!

2½ OUNCES APPLE CINNAMON BOURBON (PAGE 29)

1 OUNCE PASSION FRUIT NECTAR

LYNN'S LEMONADE (PAGE 32)

1 STAR FRUIT SLICE, FOR GARNISH

Fill a pilsner or Collins glass with crushed ice. Add the bourbon and passion fruit nectar, and top with lemonade. Transfer to a cocktail shaker, shake for a few seconds, and return the mixture to the glass. Slice a star fruit into ¼-inch-thick sections, and on one of them make a small cut between two of the points. Pierce the star fruit slice with a paper parasol, place the fruit on the rim of the glass, and serve with a straw.

COCONUT CUCUMBER MOJITO

SERVES 1

This cocktail is one of the most popular mojitos at the Hula Hut. Cool, refreshing cucumber sourced locally and fresh mint grown onsite make it delicious and dangerously smooth. Sip it slowly and savor the flavor.

5 MINT LEAVES

3 LIME WHEELS

3 CUCUMBER WHEELS, PLUS MORE FOR GARNISH, IF DESIRED

½ OUNCE AGAVE NECTAR

2 OUNCES COCONUT RUM

CLUB SODA, CHILLED

1 SPRIG MINT, FOR GARNISH

1 (4-INCH) SUGARCANE STALK, FOR GARNISH

Place the mint, lime, cucumber, and agave nectar in a large rocks glass. Muddle gently. Fill the glass with crushed ice and add the coconut rum. Transfer the contents of the glass to a cocktail shaker and shake for a few seconds. Pour the cocktail back into the glass and top with a splash of club soda. Garnish with the mint sprig, sugarcane stalk, and a few cucumber wheels, if you like.

SUGARCANE

A kind of tropical grass, sugarcane is the world's largest production crop. Some 80 percent of commercial sugar comes from sugarcane, which is harvested in more than 90 countries today, primarily Brazil. Portuguese colonists first planted it there in the early 1500s, establishing the first large-scale production of the crop. Over the course of the sixteenth century, the demand and price for sugarcane skyrocketed because sugar had replaced honey as the preferred sweetener for European recipes, particularly jams and jellies. By the middle of the seventeenth century, mills popped up throughout Brazil as the country established itself as the world's premier sugarcane producer. But that success met with competition, especially from the Caribbean, where various islands sought a piece of the lucrative sugar trade. Sugarcane remains a staple in the tropics as well as in tropical drinks everywhere. It still grows in abundance in southern Louisiana, too. Stalks of raw sugarcane, used in some tiki cocktails, add a layer of enjoyment because you can chew the stalks to extract the sweet juice.

FORTALEZA KIWI CAIPIRINHA

SERVES 1

Many years ago, my friend Marco rented a place on the northeast coast of Brazil in Fortaleza, the windsurfing and kite surfing capital of the world, where spectacular dunes cascade onto a white sandy beach. Our daily menu often consisted of freshly caught fish purchased from local fishermen along with an abundance of coconuts, kiwis, limes, and, of course, cachaça, the Brazilian liquor made from fresh sugarcane juice— a real bargain then and there at just a couple of dollars per liter. Brazil's national cocktail, the caipirinha, makes good use of cachaça, and I re-created the drink with a sweet and sexy kiwi twist. Kiwi fruit contains more vitamin C than oranges and has a wonderful tangy sweetness. Sip a Fortaleza Kiwi Caipirinha while watching the sun sink into the sea.

½ KIWI, PLUS ½ KIWI WHEEL FOR GARNISH

1 LIME

2 TABLESPOONS SUGAR

2½ OUNCES CACHAÇA (SEE NOTE)

1 LIME WHEEL, FOR GARNISH

Using a vegetable peeler or paring knife, remove the skin from the kiwi fruit. Cut the kiwi into small chunks and place in a rocks glass. Roll the lime on a hard surface to release the juices, and cut it into eight wedges. Place the lime wedges in the glass, add the sugar, and muddle well. Add some crushed ice and the cachaça and shake vigorously. Use your hips and serve with a wink. Garnish with a lime wheel and a half kiwi wheel.

NOTE: If your local liquor store doesn't carry cachaça, use an aged Jamaican rum. I prefer Appleton Estate aged rum.

GIN BEACH BREEZE

Gin Beach lies beyond Montauk's jetty, surrounded by water, where few tourists venture. The peaceful beauty of this secluded spot is unmatched, and a chilled pitcher of this delicious cocktail is like the refreshing ocean breeze in liquid form.

8 OUNCES PREMIUM DRY GIN

8 OUNCES POMEGRANATE JUICE

6 OUNCES GRAPEFRUIT JUICE

2 OUNCES FRESH LIME JUICE

1 OUNCE PINEAPPLE JUICE

4 LIME WEDGES, FOR GARNISH

In 32-ounce container or pitcher, combine the gin and juices. Secure with a lid and lightly shake. Refrigerate for up to 3 days or, better yet, put the container in a cooler packed with ice and head to the beach!

When ready to serve, fill four highball glasses with ice, shake the mixture lightly again, and divide evenly among the glasses. Garnish each with a lime wedge and enjoy.

GIN BELLINI

SERVES 1

This drink is an excellent choice for a sophisticated summer brunch and pairs perfectly with oysters, fresh fruits, and light crêpes. Giuseppe Cipriani concocted this sparkling wine cocktail in the early 1900s while tending bar in Venice, Italy, naming it after Italian Renaissance painter Giovanni Bellini. The original calls specifically for Prosecco, although some establishments prefer to use Champagne or Champagne-style sparkling wines. You can use either. I prefer to add the sweet tropical flavors of mango and agave nectar. For an added twist, this recipe uses a garnish of thyme instead of the standard cherry or strawberry. However you make it, always serve this refreshing cocktail cold.

1 OUNCE BOODLES GIN OR OTHER PREMIUM DRY GIN

¼ OUNCE CAMPARI

¼ OUNCE MANGO NECTAR

1 TEASPOON AGAVE NECTAR OR LIGHT BROWN SUGAR

PROSECCO OR DRY SPARKLING WINE

1 SPRIG THYME, FOR GARNISH

In a cocktail shaker filled with ice, combine the gin, Campari, mango nectar, and agave nectar. Shake for about 10 seconds, then strain into a chilled champagne flute. Top with some Prosecco and garnish with the thyme sprig.

GREAT WHITE BITE

SERVES 1

The waters off Montauk teem with a variety of sharks, including the blue, mako, thresher, and infamous great white. On August 6, 1986, legendary Montauk shark fisherman Frank Mundus landed the world's largest great white shark aboard the Cricket II. The shark tipped the scales at 3,427 pounds! Before the Hula Hut opened, my friend Carl asked me to set up my traveling tiki bar on the dock at his marina during one of the local shark tournaments. I wanted to create a new twist on the traditional margarita, and it had to have a bite—a great white bite! Another friend, David—a local farmer known as the "Pepper Guru"—sold me some jalapeños and fresh cilantro, and off I went. After some experimenting, the Great White Bite took shape. The next day, I pulled into the marina and served up the concoction, and the Great White Bite became an instant hit. Locals call it the Shark Bite Margarita, and it's still a top seller at the Hula Hut.

1 LIME	LYNN'S LEMONADE (PAGE 32)
2 OUNCES SILVER TEQUILA	KOSHER SALT, FOR RIMMING
¾ OUNCE COINTREAU	1 SPRIG CILANTRO, FOR GARNISH (OPTIONAL)
1 TEASPOON CUCUMBER, CILANTRO & JALAPEÑO PUREE (PAGE 23)	

Slice the lime in half and squeeze the juice from one of the halves into a cocktail shaker filled with ice. Slice the other half into wedges and set aside. Add the tequila, Cointreau, and puree to the shaker. Top with lemonade and shake for about 10 seconds while dancing to salsa music. Spread some salt over a small plate. Run a lime wedge around the rim of a margarita or rocks glass, then dip it into the salt to coat. Strain the mixture from the shaker into the glass. Garnish with a lime wedge or cilantro sprig.

GUAVA MINT CAIPIRINHA

SERVES 1

The guava, a pear-shaped, greenish-yellow tropical fruit, grows in Mexico, South America, and parts of Asia. This sweet and delicious fruit is loaded with vitamin C and fiber. It's good for your skin, it helps lower blood pressure, and because it's high in fiber and lower in sugar than most tropical fruits, it's great for weight loss. It's also delicious when paired with mint and cachaça, as you'll see when you try this cocktail. For best results, play some smooth Brazilian jazz in the background while you make this drink.

3 OR 4 MINT LEAVES

**3 LIME SLICES, ABOUT
1/8 INCH THICK**

**1/4 OUNCE AGAVE NECTAR,
OR 1½ TEASPOONS
BROWN SUGAR**

**2 OUNCES CACHAÇA
(SEE NOTE, PAGE 51)**

1½ OUNCES GUAVA NECTAR

1 SPRIG MINT, FOR GARNISH

Place the mint leaves in the bottom of a cocktail shaker. Cover them with the lime slices and gently muddle. Add the agave nectar, cachaça, and guava nectar. Add ice and shake for about 15 seconds. Strain into a rocks glass filled with ice and garnish with the mint sprig

HANALEI BAY BREEZE

Hanalei Bay sits on the north shore of Kaua'i, the oldest of the Hawaiian Islands. It's known as the Garden Isle, and it's one of the most magical places on Earth. This drink will take you there.

4 OUNCES HULA HUT HULA JUICE SPICED COCONUT RUM (OR A MIX OF 2 OUNCES COCONUT RUM, 1 OUNCE LIGHT RUM, AND 1 OUNCE SPICED RUM)

1 OUNCE PREMIUM DARK RUM

4 OUNCES FRESH PINEAPPLE JUICE

4 OUNCES POMEGRANATE JUICE

1 OUNCE FRESH LIME JUICE

4 TRAVERSE CITY CHERRY BOMBS (PAGE 13)

2 PINEAPPLE WEDGES, FOR GARNISH

In a large cocktail shaker, combine the spiced coconut rum, ½ ounce of the dark rum, and the pineapple, pomegranate, and lime juices. Add ice and shake for about 10 seconds. Fill two Collins glasses with ice and strain the cocktail into the glasses, dividing it evenly. Float ¼ ounce of dark rum atop each cocktail. Spear a cherry, then a pineapple wedge, then a second cherry with a cocktail pick or paper parasol, then rest one on the edge of each glass and serve.

TRAVERSE CITY CHERRIES

At the base of Lake Michigan's Grand Traverse Bay lies Traverse City, Michigan. About 20 miles west you'll find Sleeping Bear Dunes National Lakeshore, a natural formation with miles of sandy beaches and "perched dunes" created by glaciers towering 450 feet above Lake Michigan's northwest coast. This part of Michigan's Lower Peninsula is not only a beautiful spot for outdoor recreation in both summer and winter—among its beautiful beaches, picturesque peninsulas, and surrounding countryside—but its relatively mild climate and fertile soils make it perfect for growing many varieties of fruit. Traverse City is known as the Cherry Capital of the World, with more than four million tart cherry trees that produce 75 percent of the tart cherries grown in America. In a state with more freshwater coastline than any other—where you're never more than 6 miles from water—boaters stock their coolers with tiki drinks all summer long. Even on the Great Lakes, tiki culture is alive and well!

HIBISCUS LEMONADE

SERVES 1

I was inspired to create this cocktail after spending a winter in the Virgin Islands. Keep a large jar of it in the fridge to cool you off on a hot tropical day.

½ CUP BOILING WATER

1 HIBISCUS TEA BAG

1 TABLESPOON RAW HONEY

2 OUNCES HULA HUT LÉ HUKILAU LEMONGRASS & GINGER VODKA

2 OUNCES LYNN'S LEMONADE (PAGE 32)

⅛ TEASPOON MINCED FRESH GINGER

1 EDIBLE ORCHID OR HIBISCUS FLOWER, FOR GARNISH

Pour the boiling water into a large cup or mug and add the tea bag and honey. Let steep for several minutes. Cool to room temperature and refrigerate for up to 3 days before using.

In a cocktail shaker, combine the chilled hibiscus tea, vodka, lemonade, and ginger. Fill with ice and shake for about 10 seconds. Strain into a medium mason jar or pint glass filled with ice. Garnish with an edible orchid and serve with a straw.

HOT BASIL & BERRY LEMONADE

SERVES 1

This cocktail will take your mouth on a flavorful joyride. It's everything I love in one glass and perfect on a hot summer afternoon. Some say that it's the heat of this drink that cools you off. You'll have to try one or two to find out for sure.

1½ OUNCES VODKA

¼ OUNCE GREEN CHARTREUSE

2½ OUNCES HOT BASIL & BERRY PUREE (PAGE 25)

LYNN'S LEMONADE (PAGE 32)

3 LARGE BLACKBERRIES, FOR GARNISH

1 SPRIG BASIL, FOR GARNISH

1 JALAPEÑO SPEAR, SEEDED (IF DESIRED), FOR GARNISH (OPTIONAL)

Fill a Collins glass with ice. Add the vodka, Chartreuse, and puree and top with the lemonade. Transfer to a cocktail shaker, shake, and return to the glass. Repeat.

Garnish with the blackberry, basil sprig, and jalapeño spear, if desired.

HOT MANGO MAMACITA

SERVES 1

Holy mother of mango, this is one spicy cocktail! The secret is the Hot Mango Puree, which contains jalapeño and sriracha, the popular Asian hot sauce made from chile peppers, vinegar, garlic, sugar, and salt. Add more or less depending on your comfort level. The cool crispness of the lime juice, lemonade, and ice will help balance the heat.

2 OUNCES PREMIUM SILVER TEQUILA

½ OUNCE COINTREAU

¼ OUNCE FRESH LIME JUICE

3 OUNCES HOT MANGO PUREE (PAGE 26)

KOSHER SALT, FOR RIMMING (OPTIONAL)

LYNN'S LEMONADE (PAGE 32)

1 LIME TWIST OR WEDGE, FOR GARNISH

1 JALAPEÑO SLICE, FOR GARNISH (OPTIONAL)

EDIBLE ORCHIDS, FOR GARNISH (OPTIONAL)

Fill a pint glass with ice. Add the tequila, Cointreau, lime juice, and puree. Transfer to a shaker and shake for about 5 seconds. Salt the rim of the glass if you like. Return the drink to the glass and top with the lemonade. Garnish with a lime twist. For that extra wow, add a jalapeño slice and edible orchids.

HOT PINEAPPLE SAKE SPRITZER

SERVES 1

You won't find sake in tiki drinks often, but sake did appear in Polynesian and then tiki culture around World War II, when a number of the Pacific islands housed American military bases on the war's eastern front. Japanese fighter pilots, known as kamikazes— from the Japanese words for "divine wind" and for which the popular kamikaze drink is named— drank sake prior to carrying out their missions. This cold cocktail is refreshing and smooth—but don't be fooled. This one might just knock your sake off!

1 OUNCE PINEAPPLE JALAPEÑO VODKA (PAGE 33)

SPLASH OF PINEAPPLE JUICE

1 OUNCE DRY SAKE

CLUB SODA, CHILLED

1 PINEAPPLE WEDGE, FOR GARNISH

Fill a Collins glass with crushed ice. Add the vodka and the pineapple juice. Add the sake and top with club soda. Garnish with a pineapple wedge and serve with a straw.

HOT PINK DRINK

SERVES 1

The refreshing sensation of cucumber and the heat of the chiles tastefully balance with the cool, fresh mint. This cocktail will definitely take your taste buds on an interesting ride to Thailand's part of the Pacific Rim. Take a sip, close your eyes, and feel the warm breezes of Phuket. This great summer drink will pleasantly surprise your guests.

2½ OUNCES CUCUMBER CHILE VODKA (PAGE 30)

5 OUNCES PINK LEMONADE (PAGE 34)

2 OR 3 SPEARMINT OR MINT LEAVES

1 LEMON WHEEL, FOR GARNISH

1 SPRIG SPEARMINT OR MINT, FOR GARNISH

Fill a highball glass with ice and add the vodka and pink lemonade. Tear the spearmint leaves to release their flavor and add them to the drink. (Don't muddle them.) Stir with a straw and garnish with a lemon wheel and the mint sprig.

> NOTE: This cocktail is dedicated to Tracy and Joy, two of my dearest friends, both of whom are breast cancer survivors. It's also dedicated to those who lost the battle and to the brave women around the world who continue the fight.

HUKILAU LEMONADE

Hukilau is an ancient Hawaiian form of fishing using a cast net. Several fishermen drag the net along the shore in waist-deep water while family and friends gather on the beach to sing traditional *hukilau* songs to inspire the fishermen and celebrate the catch. A modern day *hukilau* celebration takes place every year in Fort Lauderdale, Florida. Coconuts filled with Polynesian concoctions and decorated with drink umbrellas abound as the music of Martin Denny and Dick Dale fills the warm air. Put it on your bucket list, and make a bucket of this cocktail to share when you're there.

2½ OUNCES HULA HUT LÉ
HUKILAU LEMONGRASS
& GINGER VODKA

1 SMALL SCOOP OF LEMON
SORBET (ABOUT ⅓ CUP)

LYNN'S LEMONADE (PAGE 32)

1 LEMON WHEEL,
FOR GARNISH

BROWN SUGAR, FOR GARNISH

1 SPRIG THYME, FOR GARNISH

Fill a large brandy snifter with crushed ice. Add the vodka and sorbet, and top with the lemonade. Coat the lemon wheel in brown sugar. Garnish the drink with the lemon wheel along with the sprig of thyme. Then lie back in a hammock and celebrate catching some rays.

LOTTA COLADA

The classic Puerto Rican piña colada inspired this cocktail, which is a huge hit at the Hula Hut. This version of the drink is shaken, and you can't have just one.

1½ OUNCES PREMIUM SILVER RUM

½ OUNCE DARK CRÈME DE CACAO

½ OUNCE FRANGELICO OR OTHER HAZELNUT LIQUEUR

2 OUNCES COCO LÓPEZ CREAM OF COCONUT

2½ OUNCES PINEAPPLE JUICE

1 DRUNKEN PINEAPPLE WEDGE (PAGE 18), FOR GARNISH

1 TRAVERSE CITY CHERRY BOMB (PAGE 13), FOR GARNISH

In a small hurricane glass (about 12 ounces), combine the rum, crème de cacao, Frangelico, cream of coconut, and pineapple juice. Fill to the top with crushed ice. Transfer to a cocktail shaker and shake for about 3 seconds (see Note). Return the mixture to the glass. Garnish with the pineapple wedge, drop in the cherry, and serve with a straw.

> **NOTE:** You can also blend this cocktail and serve it frozen. Instead of shaking it, transfer the ingredients to a blender and blend for about 20 seconds, until smooth. Garnish and serve as above.

MANDARIN & FENNEL ICED TEA

SERVES 1

Cultivated in the Mediterranean, fennel appears widely in Italian and Greek cuisine. The herb has an anise-like flavor but is sweeter and more aromatic. Fennel is said to promote bone health and prevent heart disease, and it has been used in the preparation of absinthe since the late eighteenth century. (Absinthe originally was served as a medicinal elixir.) Fennel also helps create an extremely crisp and refreshing combination when paired with mandarin orange and lemon, as you'll taste in this delicious summertime drink.

½ CUP BOILING WATER

1 MANDARIN ORANGE TEA BAG

1 TABLESPOON RAW HONEY

1½ OUNCES DRY GIN

1 OUNCE LYNN'S LEMONADE (PAGE 32)

2 OUNCES FENNEL ORANGE PUREE (PAGE 25)

1 ORANGE WHEEL, FOR GARNISH

1 SPRIG FENNEL FRONDS, FOR GARNISH

Pour the water into a large cup or mug, and add the tea bag and honey. Let steep for several minutes. Remove the tea bag and cool the tea to room temperature. This can be refrigerated for up to 3 days.

Fill a medium mason jar (about 12 ounces) with ice. Add the chilled tea, gin, lemonade, and puree. Stir, then garnish with the orange wheel and the fennel sprig.

MANGO, MINT & RUM SPRITZER

SERVES 1

This cocktail is refreshingly simple, but I bet you didn't know that mangoes are said to prevent cancer, lower cholesterol, fight acne, and even increase your sex drive. This delicious fruit is loaded with vitamins A and E, which are crucial to maintaining eyesight and a healthy alkaline balance. The fresh mint, grown on site at Lynn's Hula Hut, aids digestion and beautifully balances the rum and mango. Let's toast to your health!

2 OUNCES APPLETON ESTATE RUM OR OTHER GOLDEN RUM

2 OUNCES MANGO & MINT PUREE (PAGE 26)

1 OR 2 DASHES BITTERS

CLUB SODA, CHILLED

1 LIME TWIST OR WHEEL, FOR GARNISH

1 SPRIG MINT, FOR GARNISH

1 MANGO SPEAR, FOR GARNISH (OPTIONAL)

Fill a Collins glass with ice. Add the rum, puree, and bitters, then top with club soda. Garnish with lime twist, mint sprig, and mango spear, if desired, and serve with a straw.

MAYAN CHOCOLATE

SERVES 1

Montauk lies just 20 miles from Connecticut, meaning it experiences those long and brutal New England winters. One winter, to escape the cold I headed down to the Mayan Riviera. At the time, it still had dirt roads, dense jungle, and the occasional watering hole with swings instead of barstools. On a blissfully hot day, I happened upon a tiny Mayan family's grilled chicken stand where the owner, Jorge, grilled up the most amazing split chickens while his wife, Maria, and their four children plucked the animals for the next meal. After the most succulent dish of grilled chicken made with a red pepper dry rub, rice, beans, and pico de gallo, I fell in love. Before I left, Maria's grandmother gave me the most amazing gift: homemade Mexican chocolate. This delicacy—crafted long before artisanal chocolate makers copied the idea—changed the way I look at cooking. That unexpected sensation of sweet and spicy tasted of pure genius. This is my version of that game-changing Mayan chocolate bar.

3 OUNCES PINEAPPLE JALAPEÑO VODKA (PAGE 33)	**1 PINEAPPLE WEDGE, FOR GARNISH**
1 OUNCE DARK CRÈME DE CACAO	**DARK CHOCOLATE SYRUP, FOR GARNISH**

In a cocktail shaker, combine the vodka and crème de cacao and dry shake (no ice) for a few seconds. Pour into an ice-filled rocks glass. Dip only the point of the pineapple wedge in chocolate syrup. Then pierce the wedge with a bamboo skewer and lay it across the top of the glass.

> NOTE: To serve this cocktail as a dessert martini, rub the edge of a martini glass with a slice of jalapeño and rim with brown sugar. Serve straight up.

MAYAN SUNRISE

In the 1990s, Mexico's Mayan Coast was still very rural. But a friend and I motorbiked down to Belize without a care in the world. Every so often, we hung a sharp left to find a secluded beach, where we cooled off in the sparkling waters of the Caribbean. To our delight, we discovered a few amazing casitas on the beach that served tequila and fresh sandia (watermelon juice). Drinks made there with fresh pineapples, coconut, and mangoes changed the way I looked at cocktails. One of my favorite memories from that trip is sitting on the beach in Tulum and watching the sun rise over the water. The beauty of that spiritual experience served as my inspiration for this cocktail. You should never watch the sunrise alone, so this recipe serves four.

9 OUNCES COCO LOCO INFUSION (PAGE 30)

7 OUNCES PINEAPPLE JUICE

7 OUNCES POMEGRANATE JUICE

2 OUNCES FRESH LIME JUICE

4 DASHES GRENADINE

4 PINEAPPLE WEDGES, FOR GARNISH

4 TRAVERSE CITY CHERRY BOMBS (PAGE 13), FOR GARNISH

In a large pitcher, combine the Coco Loco Infusion and all of the juices. Stir and refrigerate for at least 1 hour.

Fill four large rocks glasses with crushed ice. Stir the chilled mixture again and divide it evenly among the glasses. Add a dash of grenadine to each cocktail and garnish each with a pineapple wedge and a cherry.

> **NOTE:** You also can batch this drink by making it in a large jar with a lid. Prepare it the same way, but shake it instead of stirring. It will keep in the refrigerator for up to 3 days.

MELLOW YELLOW

This cocktail evokes the tropical climes of Jamaica, where I tasted ginger beer for the first time at a little beach shack in Negril. The sweetness of the pineapple nicely crowns the interplay of the spicy ginger and the smooth vanilla.

2 OUNCES HULA HUT LÉ TAHITIAN VANILLA & PINEAPPLE VODKA

1 OUNCE PINEAPPLE JUICE

1 TEASPOON FRESH LIME JUICE

GINGER BEER

1 PINEAPPLE WEDGE, FOR GARNISH

1 VANILLA BEAN, FOR GARNISH

In a highball glass filled with ice, combine the vodka, pineapple juice, and lime juice, then top with ginger beer, filling the glass to the rim. Garnish with the pineapple wedge and vanilla bean.

> **NOTE:** Jamaica's spices and fruits have influenced many tiki drinks over the years. Cucumber juice, ginger beer, lime and mango juices, and pineapple soda all come from Jamaica, and all will elevate your tiki cocktails to deliciously new levels. Jamaica is also renowned for its rums, including Appleton Estate, the oldest sugar estate and distillery on the island. Appleton's world-class rums find their way into a variety of cocktails, from Jamaica's own Planter's Punch to classic tiki drinks like the Zombie (page 169).

TAHITIAN SNAKE CHARMER

This concoction takes you on a magic carpet ride. The natural sweetness of Tahitian vanilla and pineapple, the savory sage, the smoky essence of the mezcal, and fresh lime juice creates a beautifully balanced and surprisingly delicious cocktail.

TAJÍN, FOR RIMMING THE
GLASS (OPTIONAL)

1½ OUNCES HULA HUT
LÉ TAHITIAN VANILLA &
PINEAPPLE VODKA

½ OUNCE DOS
HOMBRES MEZCAL

1½ OUNCES
PINEAPPLE JIUCE

¼ OUNCE FRESH LIME JUICE

⅛ TEASPOON DRIED SAGE

DEHYDRATED LIME WHEEL,
FOR GARNISH (OPTIONAL)

PINEAPPLE WEDGE, FOR
GARNISH (OPTIONAL)

Rim a rocks glass with Tajín (optional). Add all the liquid ingredients into a shaker, dry shake, then strain into a rocks glass filled with fresh ice. Garnish with a dehydrated lime wheel and pineapple wedge (optional).

MONTAUK MARINE COOLER

SERVES 1

A wild group of women on a bachelorette party bar crawl, sporting sexy sailor outfits and phallic party favors, wandered into Lynn's Hula Hut one sunny afternoon. Some of the local fishermen are out at sea for weeks at a time, so this could have been a dangerous situation, but the women held their own and everyone had a great time. As we say, "What happens at Lynn's Hula Hut *never* stays at Lynn's Hula Hut!" Later the girls asked me to create a refreshing cocktail for them, and its name is a nod to their outfits. This drink encompasses everything summertime: the deep blue of the sea, fresh watermelon, and the aroma of the basil that reminds me of the sweet smell of privet, which grows in abundance on the East End. I swear like a sailor that you'll love this cooler!

1¼ OUNCES PATRÓN OR OTHER SILVER TEQUILA

1¼ OUNCES TITO'S VODKA

¼ OUNCE BLUE CURAÇAO

LYNN'S LEMONADE (PAGE 32)

WATERMELON & BASIL PUREE (PAGE 27)

1 ORANGE WHEEL, FOR GARNISH

1 WATERMELON WEDGE, FOR GARNISH (OPTIONAL)

1 FRESH BASIL LEAF, FOR GARNISH (OPTIONAL)

Fill a Collins or large martini glass with ice. Add the tequila, vodka, and blue curaçao. Add enough lemonade to fill the glass three-quarters full. Transfer to a cocktail shaker and shake for a few seconds. Return the mixture to the glass and top with the puree. Garnish with the orange wheel or lean into the flavors of the puree and garnish with the watermelon wedge and the basil leaf, speared on a bamboo skewer.

THE SAMOAN

SERVES 1

In Denver, my girlfriends and I would attend the annual Ruggerfest (or the Eye Candy Fest, as we fondly called it) in Aspen. This annual rugby tournament draws thousands of spectators and partygoers to watch teams annihilate one another and then drink and sing tribal songs. Many of the players come from Tonga, Fiji, and Samoa, where rugby is a hugely popular sport. This drink is dedicated to the fond memory of Ben Masoe and the boys performing the haka in their underwear at 3:00 a.m.

2 OUNCES COCONUT RUM

½ OUNCE FRANGELICO OR OTHER HAZELNUT LIQUEUR

3 OUNCES ORANGE JUICE

3 OUNCES POMEGRANATE JUICE

1 SQUEEZE FRESH LIME JUICE

1 ORANGE WHEEL, FOR GARNISH

1 EDIBLE ORCHID, FOR GARNISH

1 LIME TWIST, FOR GARNISH (OPTIONAL)

Fill a Collins glass with ice. Add the rum, Frangelico, orange juice, pomegranate juice, and lime juice. Transfer to a cocktail shaker and shake for a few seconds. Return the mixture to the glass and garnish with the orange wheel, orchid, and lime twist, if desired.

> **NOTE:** The haka is a traditional, ancestral war dance originally performed by warriors before battle to intimidate enemies or opponents. They would stomp their feet and scream and shout to announce their power and strength. This powerful dance, with its celebrated war cry, is also used to welcome important guests or to pay homage at a significant event, like a funeral.

PAPAYA BOURBON CIDER

Papaya is a must-have for tiki cocktails. This soft, buttery tropical fruit, which originated in Mexico and spread throughout the Caribbean, provides plenty of sweetness along with a wonderful orange hue. Columbus prized the fruit when he sailed the globe. Papayas are rich in vitamin C and fiber, and they contain enzymes that may help treat allergies and injuries. You can enjoy this cocktail all year round. This is the warm-weather version, but you can serve it with warm cider during the holidays.

2 OUNCES APPLE CINNAMON BOURBON (PAGE 29)	**2 TO 3 OUNCES CHILLED APPLE CIDER**
3 OUNCES PAPAYA NECTAR	**1 LEMON WHEEL, FOR GARNISH**
¼ OUNCE AGAVE NECTAR	**2 CINNAMON STICKS, FOR GARNISH**
1 OUNCE FRESH LEMON JUICE	

Fill a 12-ounce mason jar with ice. Add the bourbon infusion, papaya nectar, agave nectar, and lemon juice. Top with the apple cider and pour it into a cocktail shaker. Shake for about 3 seconds. Return the mixture to the mason jar and garnish with the lemon wheel and cinnamon sticks. Serve with a straw.

ROSEMARY LEMONADE

SERVES 1

Lois, the dearest gin snob I've known, proudly claims to have sixty years of expertise in this field. "Life is about balance," she says. One day she asked if I had any recipes with gin, so I served her this cocktail. As she lifted the glass to her lips, a gentle smile washed over her face as she inhaled. She sipped and said, "Lovely." If you're not a gin lover, maybe it's time to give it another try. Gin, made with juniper berries and other botanicals, such as flowers, roots, fruits, and seeds, is the perfect spirit to infuse into tiki drinks like Rosemary Lemonade. The gin's smooth, cheerful crispness balances out the sweetness of the lemonade and syrup while complementing the subtle flavors of the rosemary.

2½ OUNCES BOMBAY SAPPHIRE OR OTHER DRY GIN (SEE NOTE)

2 OUNCES LYNN'S LEMONADE (PAGE 32)

1 OUNCE ROSEMARY LEMON SYRUP (PAGE 22)

1 SPRIG ROSEMARY, FOR GARNISH

1 LEMON WHEEL, FOR GARNISH

In a cocktail shaker filled with ice, combine the gin, lemonade, and syrup. Shake for 10 seconds, then strain into a rocks glass filled with ice. Garnish with the rosemary sprig and lemon wheel.

NOTE: For a different and equally refreshing take on this cocktail, try making it with Hendrick's gin, which features soft botanical notes of cooling cucumbers and soothing rose petals.

SANTORINI SPRITZER

SERVES 1

This cocktail, made with ouzo, a Greek aperitif flavored with anise and other herbs, is dedicated to Uncle Michael Alexandrou, an international businessman and world traveler, and the Dapontes family, a lovely and wild Greek family I grew up with. They hail from the island of Kythera, said to be the birthplace of Aphrodite, goddess of love. The island served as a crossroads for sailors and merchants, creating a melting pot of cultures influenced by the Ottoman and Venetian empires, clearly evident in the island's architecture. Lemons, oranges, and fennel all grow here, where the shimmering Aegean Sea caresses beautiful beaches dotted with thatched tiki bars. Polynesian culture has made its way even to the Greek islands! Enjoy this refreshing cocktail as Apollo's chariot sinks into the sea.

1 OUNCE OUZO

1 OUNCE LIMONCELLO

2 OUNCES FENNEL ORANGE PUREE (PAGE 25)

TONIC WATER, CHILLED

1 MANDARIN ORANGE WEDGE WITH PEEL, FOR GARNISH

Fill a Collins glass with ice. Add the ouzo, limoncello, and puree. Top with tonic water. Stir and then garnish with the orange wedge.

SEASCAPE ALMOND SLUSH

SERVES 1

The Seascape, a 14-room boutique motel on Singer Island, Florida, is owned by two remarkable hosts who inspired the Almond Slush. Thanks for the hospitality, Alicia and Hagan. This one's for you!

¾ OUNCE LIGHT RUM

¾ OUNCE SPICED RUM

½ OUNCE AMARETTO

⅛ OUNCE COINTREAU

1½ OUNCES MANGO NECTAR

1½ OUNCES PINEAPPLE JUICE

1½ DASHES STIRRINGS
OR OTHER BLOOD
ORANGE BITTERS

½ MANDARIN ORANGE,
PEELED AND SEGMENTED

1 EDIBLE ORCHID,
FOR GARNISH

1 MANGO SPEAR,
FOR GARNISH

In a blender, combine the light rum, spiced rum, amaretto, Cointreau, mango nectar, pineapple juice, bitters, mandarin orange, and 1 cup of ice. Blend on high until smooth. Pour into a chilled highball glass and garnish with the orchid and mango spear.

TAHITI 5-OH!

SERVES 2

You can't mention tiki without mentioning Hawai'i. For twelve seasons, from 1968 to 1980, the popular *Hawaii Five-O* TV show was shot on location in the Aloha State, proving that a police procedural set in a tropical paradise can survive just like good tiki drinks, which were enormously popular during the show's run. Perhaps not coincidentally, the tiki craze reemerged along with the reboot of the series in 2010. A perfect blend of five ingredients makes this tropical delight that playfully refers to the TV show a great refreshing summer cocktail. This recipe serves two, because it's always better to have a partner in crime. Just don't get into trouble after you have one. Otherwise, "Book 'em, Danno!"

2½ OUNCES HULA HUT LÉ TAHITIAN VANILLA & PINEAPPLE VODKA

2½ OUNCES COCONUT RUM

½ OUNCE BLUE CURAÇAO

3 OUNCES COCO LÓPEZ OR OTHER CREAM OF COCONUT

6 OUNCES PINEAPPLE JUICE

2 DRUNKEN PINEAPPLE WEDGES (PAGE 18), FOR GARNISH

In a blender, combine the vodka, rum, curaçao, cream of coconut, pineapple juice, and 2 cups ice. Blend on high until smooth. Divide between two Collins glasses. Garnish with the pineapple wedges and serve with paper umbrellas and straws.

TUTU'S SLUSH & FLUSH

Tutu is an endearing Hawaiian term for grandmother, but it can refer to both genders. Dried plums are an excellent natural source of vitamins and fiber, and are great for skin and bone health, but most people think of their grandparents when they hear the word *prune*. Years ago, while spending the winter months in South Florida, I met many wonderful grandparents from all over the world. Since they and my grandmother Fiorita served as the inspiration for this cocktail, I asked them to taste test it. No one guessed that prune juice is one of the ingredients. They absolutely loved it, so this cocktail is dedicated respectfully to all of the wise ones who lovingly paved the way for us.

2½ OUNCES HULA HUT LÉ HUKILAU LEMONGRASS & GINGER VODKA

3½ OUNCES PRUNE JUICE

½ OUNCE AGAVE NECTAR

JUICE OF ½ LEMON

1 LEMON WHEEL, FOR GARNISH

In a cocktail shaker, combine the vodka, juice, agave nectar, and lemon juice. Add some ice and shake for about 10 seconds. Strain and pour into a martini glass half filled with crushed ice. Garnish with the lemon wheel and serve immediately.

VERY BERRY BRAZIL

First distilled by the Portuguese in the 1500s, cachaça is a spirit distilled from sugar cane and aged in wood barrels for up to twelve months. It's also the most widely consumed liquor in Brazil. When paired with fresh blueberries from a farmers' market and mint plucked right from the garden, the result is a perfectly balanced summer cocktail.

3 FRESH MINT LEAVES

8 TO 10 LARGE BLUEBERRIES

½ OUNCE AGAVE NECTAR

¼ OUNCE FRESH LIME JUICE

2½ OUNCES CACHAÇA

1 SPRIG MINT, FOR GARNISH

1 LIME TWIST, FOR GARNISH (OPTIONAL)

In a rocks glass, combine the mint leaves, blueberries, agave nectar, and lime juice. Muddle to release the flavor from the mint and the juice of the berries. Fill the glass with crushed ice and add the cachaça. Pour the mixture into a cocktail shaker and shake for 5 seconds. Return the cocktail to the glass and garnish with the fresh mint sprig and a lime twist if you're feeling it.

TIKITINIS

Tiki-inspired martinis are fun, sexy, and sophisticated whether served straight up in a martini glass or on the rocks. Tikitinis make a statement and set the mood for a memorable evening. When hosting an event or gathering, prepare a batch in advance and store them in sealed glass containers in the refrigerator. Then set the scene before your guests arrive. Lay banana leaves diagonally along your bar top as a tropical mat or instead of a cocktail tray. Cut your fruit and garnishes ahead of time and arrange them in coconut cups placed on the banana leaves. Put bamboo skewers, drink parasols, and straws in colorful tiki mugs. Edible tropical orchids are also a great touch. Wicker or thatched baskets can disguise an old ice bucket. Set up your chilled martini glasses on the banana leaves just before your guests arrive. Finally, you'll want to play some tunes—like Israel Kamakawiwoʻole's "Over the Rainbow" or Gabby Pahinui's "Hiʻilawe"—while you sip your tropical drinks!

CHOCOLATE DIVATINI

SERVES 1

This is the dessert version of the Raspberry Jalapeño Tikitini (page 101). The simple addition of dark chocolate liqueur transforms this cocktail into a decadent after-dinner martini. It sounds like a chick drink, but a few boat captains who shall remain nameless love it.

2 FRESH RASPBERRIES, PLUS MORE FOR GARNISH, RINSED

¼ OUNCE CHAMBORD OR OTHER RASPBERRY LIQUEUR

2 OUNCES PINEAPPLE JALAPEÑO VODKA (PAGE 33)

1 OUNCE GODIVA OR OTHER DARK CHOCOLATE LIQUEUR

SPLASH OF PINEAPPLE JUICE

1 JALAPEÑO SLICE, FOR GARNISH (OPTIONAL)

In a cocktail shaker, combine the 2 tablespoons raspberries and the Chambord and muddle the berries to release the juice. Add the vodka, chocolate liqueur, pineapple juice, and some ice. Cover and shake for 15 seconds. Strain into a chilled martini glass and garnish with a few raspberries for an added pop of freshness. For a little extra kick, add a jalapeño slice as a garnish if you like.

HOT CUCUMBER TIKITINI

SERVES 1

Recent studies are declaring the cucumber one of the world's healthiest foods. Cucumbers are said to help prevent cancer and to reduce the incidence of cardiovascular disease. Fresh cucumber extracts offer antioxidant and anti-inflammatory benefits along with an abundance of vitamin K, which is essential to building strong bones and helping prevent heart disease. This tikitini is a bit spicy, but the cucumber helps tame this delicious cocktail, which aids digestion and is tastefully smooth. Try it just before dinner.

1 OUNCE FRESH LEMON JUICE

4 CUCUMBER SLICES, ABOUT ⅛ INCH THICK

¾ OUNCE AGAVE NECTAR

2 OUNCES CUCUMBER CHILE VODKA (PAGE 30)

½ LEMON WHEEL, FOR GARNISH (OPTIONAL)

Place the lemon juice, three of the cucumber slices, and the nectar into a cocktail shaker. Muddle well. Add some ice and the vodka and shake for 10 seconds. Strain into a chilled martini glass. Float the remaining cucumber slice on top along with a half lemon wheel, if desired.

LAVENDER LEMON TIKITINI

SERVES 2

Eve wanted to get married in Brittany in an old stone church surrounded by a field of lavender. James wanted the wedding to take place in Moorea in French Polynesia. James and Eve had a prewedding cocktail party at the Hula Hut one warm spring afternoon, and, of course, Eve got her way. This cocktail pays homage to Eve's inevitable victory and serves two, in honor of James and Eve. May they drink happily ever after!

1 TABLESPOON SUGAR, FOR RIMMING

5 OUNCES HULA HUT LÉ HUKILAU LEMONGRASS & GINGER VODKA

2 OUNCES LAVENDER LEMON SYRUP (PAGE 20)

1 OUNCE FRESH LEMON JUICE

2 SPRIGS FRESH CULINARY LAVENDER (SEE NOTE), FOR GARNISH

Rim two chilled martini glasses with sugar and set aside.

In a cocktail shaker filled with ice, combine the vodka, syrup, and lemon juice and shake for 10 seconds, then strain into the chilled martini glasses, dividing it evenly. Float a lavender sprig in each cocktail.

NOTE: Although you can use most varieties of lavender in cocktails, culinary lavenders, such as English lavender, are sweeter, which increases the flavor profile of the drink. Using the fragrant leaves and stems works, but the purple flowers will give your cocktails a subtle citrus flavor. Lavender grows well in dry, sunny climes, so place a pot on your windowsill or plant some in a sunny spot in your garden.

RASPBERRY JALAPEÑO TIKITINI

SERVES 1

Raspberries are loaded with vitamin C, manganese, and fiber. They also contain a compound that may help manage obesity and type 2 diabetes. There are more than two hundred species of raspberries, but I stick to the mature red varieties like the European Red. Many years ago a dear friend gave me a jar of homemade raspberry jalapeño jam. That amazing combination of hot and sweet inspired this cocktail. The vodka infusion used in this cocktail is wonderful with the addition of sweet ripe pineapple. You can also add dark chocolate to create the perfect dessert martini, the Chocolate Divatini (page 97).

2 FRESH RASPBERRIES, PLUS MORE FOR GARNISH

½ OUNCE CHAMBORD OR OTHER RASPBERRY LIQUEUR

2 OUNCES PINEAPPLE JALAPEÑO VODKA (PAGE 33)

1½ OUNCES PINEAPPLE JUICE

Place the raspberries in a cocktail shaker. Add the Chambord and muddle the berries to release the juice. Add the vodka, pineapple juice, and some ice. Shake for about 15 seconds. Strain into a chilled martini glass and garnish with a couple of raspberries for an added pop of freshness.

THE SPEEDY RODRIGUEZ

SERVES 1

Many years ago while spending a winter in Playa del Carmen, Mexico, I frequented a little café where a Mayan man carefully stacked a pyramid of espresso cups to symbolize the Mayan pyramids of Tulum. He climbed on a stool and slowly poured a bottle of something extremely potent, like Mexican moonshine, over the coffee cups, beginning at the top and working his way down to fill every cup. Then he ignited the pyramid, and the crowd went mad! We nicknamed him Speedy Rodriguez. He did several shows a night and inspired me to create this cocktail. You can also enjoy this drink after dinner in place of an espresso.

3 OUNCES ROOM-TEMPERATURE BREWED ESPRESSO, MADE USING AN ESPRESSO MAKER OR INSTANT ESPRESSO POWDER

2 OUNCES COCO LOCO INFUSION (PAGE 30)

1 LEMON TWIST, FOR GARNISH

In a cocktail shaker, combine 1 cup of ice, the espresso, and the Coco Loco Infusion. Shake vigorously for 10 seconds, then strain into a chilled martini glass (see note). Garnish with a lemon twist.

NOTE: For more of a dessert-style presentation, rim the glass with brown sugar.

TAHITIAN LEMON DROP

SERVES 1

As the sun settles into the horizon, casting its golden amber glow, the essence of orange, pineapple, and vanilla of this sultry cocktail creates the perfect end to a perfect day.

1 LARGE LEMON

1½ TEASPOONS BROWN SUGAR, FOR RIMMING

1½ OUNCES HULA HUT LÉ TAHITIAN VANILLA & PINEAPPLE VODKA

1½ OUNCES TUACA (SEE NOTE)

⅜ OUNCE TRIPLE SEC

Slice the lemon in half crosswise. Press and strain the juice from one of the halves into a large cocktail shaker and set aside. Slice a thin wheel from the remaining half and set aside for garnish.

Rub the squeezed lemon half around the edge of a chilled martini glass, then rim with brown sugar and set aside.

Add the vodka, Tuaca, triple sec, and some ice to the shaker, and shake for 10 to 12 seconds. Strain into the prepared martini glass and float the lemon wheel atop the cocktail.

NOTE: Tuaca is an Italian citrus liqueur flavored with vanilla.

TAHITI

French Polynesia consists of 118 islands and atolls spread over five archipelagos. Millions of travelers visit each year and encounter the iconic tiki, a large wood carving representing authentic Polynesian culture. Tikis, in which the drinks originated, often mark boundaries of important and sacred sites. Polynesian clans, who considered themselves descendants of Polynesian gods, dominated the islands. Many tikis today represent these ancient gods.

Tahiti's mai tai is the most famous of the island's tropical libations. Less well known but just as delicious are the Pina Lagoon, Banana Coralia, and Maeva. If you're lucky, you may be served a cocktail garnished with a tiare flower. These sweet-scented flowers truly embody the island's spirit. But if you decide to pluck it from your glass and wear it behind your ear, make sure you understand proper placement. Wearing the tiare flower on your left ear means you're married. On your right ear signifies that you're single and searching for a mate.

TAHITI SPICE TIKITINI

SERVES 1

The Tahitian vanilla bean is the queen of vanilla. Every summer, Tahiti celebrates Vanilla Week, a delightful festival that includes opportunities to tour vanilla farms so you can learn how the world's best-quality vanilla is produced, prepared, and transformed. Tahitian vanilla has unique aromatic qualities, and its limited supply is highly sought worldwide. The Tahitian vanilla bean originated from a hybrid between West Indian and Mexican beans, resulting in a rare bean with intense fruit and floral aromas. This cocktail contains an exotic blend of vanilla, ginger, and cinnamon. When paired with citrus and chilled, it's extremely refreshing on a hot summer day.

2 OUNCES TAHITIAN BLEND INFUSION (PAGE 35)

1 OUNCE ORANGE JUICE

1 OUNCE POMEGRANATE JUICE

½ OUNCE FRESH LIME JUICE

1 ORANGE TWIST, FOR GARNISH

In a large cocktail shaker, combine the infusion, orange juice, pomegranate juice, and lime juice. Add ice and shake for 10 to 15 seconds. Strain into a chilled martini glass and garnish with the orange twist, or serve on the rocks in a wine glass with an additional lime wedge and paper parasol.

> **NOTE:** The best way to use a vanilla bean is to split the delicate pod in half, carefully exposing the seeds, which are what gives a cocktail or dish the vanilla flavor. For tropical infusions, use the entire pod.

CUCKOO FOR COCONUTS

Grown in the tropics and subtropics, coconuts are one of the most versatile fruits on the planet. (In some cultures, the coconut palm is called the tree of life and revered for its healing properties.) You can use every part of this amazing fruit, and an immature coconut contains a large amount of water that you can drink. A good coconut should feel heavy for its size. Shake the coconut. You should hear plenty of juice inside. This is the coconut water, and the more the better. Finally, inspect the outer shell of the coconut. The shell should be clean and brown. Discard any coconuts that are discolored, cracked, or don't have any water inside. To open a coconut, the best tool to use is a hammer (stay away from machetes and hatchets—you're just asking for trouble with those). With the claw of the hammer, pierce the top of the coconut (the part that looks like a miniature bowling ball with the three "eyes"). Continue to pierce the nut until the top breaks open. Be careful not to spill the delicious coconut water inside. You'll want to drink this. Remove the water and then use the hammer again to break the shell into pieces, exposing the delicious white flesh inside.

BRAZILIAN BREEZER

SERVES 1

You will absolutely flip over this cocktail. The freshness of the cucumber combined with the tropical taste of coconut will leave you wanting more. This recipe is dedicated to my Brazilian friend Adrian, whom I met years ago while vacationing in Fort Lauderdale, Florida. We met at a tiny tiki bar on a beautiful sandy beach at the Marriott Harbor Beach Resort, where Adrian was working as a bartender. He made me a refreshing concoction of muddled cucumber, rum, pineapple juice, and club soda. It was tasty, but I'm more of a tequila girl, so back in Montauk I started experimenting. With a few cucumbers muddled in my Coco Loco Infusion, the delicious and refreshing Brazilian Breezer was born!

5 CUCUMBER SLICES, ABOUT ⅛ INCH THICK

2 OUNCES PINEAPPLE JUICE

2 OUNCES COCO LOCO INFUSION (PAGE 30)

1 LIME WHEEL, FOR GARNISH (OPTIONAL)

1 PINEAPPLE WEDGE, FOR GARNISH (OPTIONAL)

In a large rocks glass, combine 4 of the cucumber slices and the pineapple juice and muddle the cucumber to release its flavor. Fill the glass with crushed ice and add the Coco Loco Infusion. Transfer to a cocktail shaker, shake for about 10 seconds, and return the cocktail to the glass. Garnish with the remaining cucumber slice, a lime wheel, and a pineapple wedge if you like.

CHILE COCONUT COOLER

SERVES 1

Chiles range from mild to scorching. In general, the smaller the pepper, the hotter it is. Be *extremely* careful when handling them, particularly in the kitchen. Use gloves—and *don't* touch your eyes afterward. The heat comes from an oily substance called capsaicin, located in yellow sacs on the inside wall of the chile pepper pod. As long as these sacs aren't broken, a hot pepper will remain mild, but biting a pepper can release its hotness. Capsaicin spreads into the pepper's seeds, so remove them to turn down the heat. Choose chiles that are glossy, firm, and free of soft spots or blemishes. Keep them in sealed plastic bags in the refrigerator for up to 1 week, or freeze them by slitting them open, removing the seeds, and placing them in freezer bags. In this cocktail, the cucumber cools the chile's heat, and the natural sweetness of the coconut water and pineapple juice offer a smooth balance. I serve this cocktail in a coconut shell drinking cup, but you can use a large rocks glass.

2 OUNCES CUCUMBER CHILE VODKA (PAGE 30)

3 OUNCES COCONUT WATER

¼ OUNCE PINEAPPLE JUICE

1 CUCUMBER SLICE, ABOUT ⅛ INCH THICK, FOR GARNISH

Combine the vodka, coconut water, and pineapple juice in a cocktail shaker with ice. Shake for about 5 seconds, then strain into a coconut shell, coconut cup, or large rocks glass filled with crushed ice. Float the cucumber slice on top and serve with a straw.

> **NOTE:** If your palate overheats from a fiery chile, never drink water to cool the burn. The best remedy is to consume dairy products, such as milk, yogurt, sour cream, or ice cream.

COCO LOCO COCKTAIL

SERVES 1

One afternoon at the Hula Hut, my friend Dianne asked me to create a cocktail with tequila and coconut, her two favorite ingredients—and mine! A petite and gorgeous mamacita, Dianne loves Latin music and a good time. Some of my customers jokingly call me "Dr. Lynn, Medicine Woman" after I've intuitively prescribed a custom cocktail for them. I just have a sense for what people want. After experimenting with several different tropical fruits, I decided to keep it simple. Just a tiny bit of pineapple juice and lime is all it took. Dianne absolutely flipped over this one, and it's now one of the top sellers at the bar. You can often catch Dianne and the gang enjoying several Coco Locos in our Zen Den. Thanks for your inspiration, chica!

2 OUNCES COCO LOCO INFUSION (PAGE 30)

2 OUNCES PINEAPPLE JUICE

¼ OUNCE FRESH LIME JUICE

1 PINEAPPLE WEDGE, FOR GARNISH

Fill a rocks glass with ice. Add the Coco Loco Infusion, pineapple juice, and lime juice. Stir, then garnish with the pineapple wedge.

COCOMINT COOLER

An exotic and stunning locale, Thailand is known for its tropical beaches, ancient ruins, and sacred shrines to the Buddha, who graces my Hula Hut as well. Thai cuisine, one of the most popular in the world, relies on fresh, local ingredients like delicious coconuts and fragrant mint, both featured in this cocktail. If you're ever in Thailand, take the time to visit the many food courts, markets, and award-winning restaurants. You can even take various culinary tours and cooking classes ... while sipping on Thai-crafted tropical cocktails like this one. The combination of coconut and mint makes it extremely refreshing.

4 MINT LEAVES

1 LIME WEDGE (PAGE 11)

¾ OUNCE AGAVE NECTAR

1½ OUNCES PREMIUM LIGHT RUM

½ OUNCE COCONUT RUM

3 OUNCES COCONUT WATER

1 SPRIG MINT, FOR GARNISH

1 COCONUT SHELL, FOR SERVING (SEE NOTE, PAGE 117; OPTIONAL)

3 LIME WHEELS, FOR GARNISH (OPTIONAL)

Place the mint leaves, lime wedge, and agave nectar in a cocktail shaker. Muddle to release the flavors from the leaves and the juice from the lime. Add the light rum, coconut rum, coconut water, and some ice. Shake for about 10 seconds. Strain into a Collins glass filled with ice. Garnish with the mint sprig and serve with a straw. Alternatively, you can serve this drink in a coconut shell garnished with lime wheels and paper parasol, if you like, for an even more tropical feel.

COCONUT WATER

Coconut water has exploded in popularity, but it's been around forever. Because it's low in calories and has no cholesterol, and one serving has more potassium than four bananas, this naturally refreshing drink adds the perfect touch to coconut cocktails. Just don't drink too much of it. Remember the movie *Castaway*? Chuck Noland—the Tom Hanks character stranded on a remote island littered with coconuts—reminds us that coconut water is a natural laxative. Coconut water also aids in weight loss because the water's naturally rich properties help suppress the appetite. Of course, we can't talk about coconut water in a cocktail book without mentioning its use as a hangover cure. Drinking coconut water after you've had one too many will settle your stomach while replacing essential electrolytes that you may have lost from dehydration (or after paying homage to the porcelain god). More important, coconut water will replace those lost minerals and vital nutrients much better than sports drinks can. If that isn't enough to convince you to drink coconut water, this natural liquid is also said to reduce blood pressure.

COCONUT COOLER

SERVES 1

For those dog days of summer, this cocktail is extremely refreshing. The gin helps cut the natural sweetness of the coconut by adding some herbal sharpness to the mixture. You'll love it.

2 OUNCES PREMIUM DRY GIN

3 OUNCES COCONUT WATER

1 OUNCE COCONUT MILK

¼ OUNCE AGAVE NECTAR

1 LIME WHEEL, FOR GARNISH

In a cocktail shaker, combine the gin, coconut water, coconut milk, and agave nectar. Add some ice and shake for about 10 seconds. Strain into a coconut shell drinking cup (see note) or large rocks glass filled with crushed ice. Garnish with the lime wheel.

NOTE: Serving cocktails in natural coconut shell drinking cups adds an authentic tropical touch to any tiki gathering. They're inexpensive, and you easily can find them online. For an intimate cocktail party or special event, order monogrammed coconut cups for your guests to take home with them. It's a nice personal touch. You can buy them from CoconutKing.com or other online retailers.

LAVENDER COCONUT COCKTAIL

SERVES 1

French Polynesia has more than fifty airports, so you can practically land on the island of your choice. No wonder almost 200,000 visitors arrive every year to frolic under the sun. Bring your sunscreen and a big appetite, because the food in French Polynesia is delicious and often prepared using local produce such as coconuts and other fresh fruits and vegetables. The islands don't have any poisonous snakes or insects, although the mosquitos bite, as might the occasional sea turtle or shark. Best to belly up to the bar and enjoy the shimmering sea from a distance with this cocktail in your hand. The flavors of lavender and coconut water perfectly balance to result in an aromatic, soothing, and hydrating cocktail. Lie back and savor this one.

2 OUNCES PREMIUM VODKA

4 OUNCES COCONUT WATER

1 OUNCE LAVENDER LEMON SYRUP (PAGE 20)

1 SPRIG FRESH LAVENDER, FOR GARNISH

In a cocktail shaker, combine the vodka, coconut water, syrup, and some ice. Shake for about 10 seconds, then strain into a coupe filled with crushed ice. Garnish with the lavender sprig and enjoy.

FROZEN DELIGHTS

Rum and pineapple juice frequently were served together in tropical climes where sugar cane and pineapples grew, but commercially viable ice didn't become available in the Caribbean until 1807. Most classic tiki cocktails are muddled and stirred or shaken—which isn't surprising because many of them originated before the blender became a common household item. Stephen Poplawski patented the first blender in 1922, the same year as the first written reference appears for that most iconic tiki drink, the piña colada. Cream of coconut didn't hit the market for several more decades, though. Ramón López Irizarry, a professor of agriculture at the University of Puerto Rico, began producing it commercially in 1954, paving the way for the piña colada recipe we know today. Tiki versions of other classic frozen drinks, such as the daiquiri and margarita, use blended fruit. Fresh fruit is always better than sugary store-bought purees or mixers, but a little bit of Coco López goes a long way. It's also better to add ice after the measured ingredients to keep it from melting too quickly.

BANANA HAMMOCK

SERVES 1

The popular and iconic 1980s television series *Miami Vice* inspired this cocktail. The drink is sexy and sophisticated and takes after the Miami Vice Cocktail—itself a combination of a Rum Runner and the piña colada—which popped up in tiki bars all over South Florida during the show's heyday. This is my twist on that retro classic.

1 RIPE BANANA

3 OUNCES HULA HUT HULA JUICE SPICED COCONUT RUM (OR A MIX OF 1½ OUNCES LIGHT RUM, 1 OUNCE COCONUT RUM, AND ½ OUNCE DARK RUM)

1 OUNCE COCO LÓPEZ OR OTHER CREAM OF COCONUT

2 OUNCES PINEAPPLE JUICE

½ OUNCE FRESH LIME JUICE

⅛ OUNCE GRENADINE

¼ CUP BLACKBERRIES

¼ CUP VANILLA ICE CREAM

Peel the banana and cut it into 4 pieces. Spear one of the end pieces with a 4-inch skewer and set aside for garnish.

In a blender, combine the remaining banana, the coconut rum, cream of coconut, pineapple juice, lime juice, grenadine, blackberries, ice cream, and 1¼ cups ice. Blend until smooth, then pour into a hurricane glass. Lay the speared banana garnish across the rim of the glass and serve with a straw.

> **NOTE:** For a nice layered effect, float a little extra dark rum atop the drink before you serve it.

CARIBBEAN COMFORT COCKTAIL

SERVES 1

This drink is off-the-charts delicious.

1 RIPE BANANA

2 OUNCES CARIBBEAN COMFORT INFUSION (PAGE 29)

1½ OUNCES PINEAPPLE JUICE

½ CUP VANILLA ICE CREAM (SEE NOTE)

½ OUNCE DARK RUM

WHIPPED CREAM

¼ TEASPOON GROUND CINNAMON

1 DRUNKEN PINEAPPLE WEDGE (PAGE 18), FOR GARNISH

Peel the banana, cut it in half lengthwise, and place one half in a blender. Add the Caribbean Comfort Infusion, pineapple juice, ice cream, and 1½ cups of ice. Blend on high until smooth, then pour into a Collins glass. Float the dark rum on top of the cocktail, and top with whipped cream and a sprinkle of cinnamon. Garnish with the pineapple wedge and the remaining banana half and serve with a straw.

> **NOTE:** You can use fat-free frozen yogurt instead of ice cream for a lighter version of the cocktail.

CARIBBEAN DREAMSICLE

SERVES 1

Don't be fooled by this surprisingly smooth and sweet treat, which I, not the ice cream man, am bringing to you.

1½ OUNCES HULA HUT LÉ TAHITIAN VANILLA & PINEAPPLE VODKA

¾ OUNCE TUACA (SEE NOTE, PAGE 103)

½ OUNCE COINTREAU

2 OUNCES ORANGE JUICE

SCANT ½ CUP VANILLA ICE CREAM

WHIPPED CREAM

1 ORANGE WEDGE, FOR GARNISH

In a blender, combine the vodka, Tuaca, Cointreau, orange juice, ice cream, and 1¼ cups of ice. Blend on high until smooth, then pour into a Collins glass. Top with whipped cream, garnish with the orange wedge, and serve with a straw.

> **NOTE:** For that extra presentation sparkle, put a sparkler in the drink, and light it before serving. Just make sure to set it on an angle so that you don't wind up with ashes in your cocktail.

HONEYDEW DAIQUIRI

I would love to come home from a hard day of work to a tall, dark, chiseled man wearing nothing but a sarong and a smile and lovingly handing me a Honeydew Daiquiri made from scratch. A girl can dream, can't she? But seriously, nothing screams "summertime" like the aroma of sweet, ripe melon. You can buy precut honeydew, but doing the prep yourself is easy. Cut the melon in half, then scoop out and discard the seeds. Use a melon baller or spoon to scoop the flesh into chunks. (See page 16 for more melon prep tips.)

½ CUP FRESH HONEYDEW MELON CHUNKS, PLUS 1 WEDGE FOR GARNISH

2 OUNCES HULA HUT LÉ TAHITIAN VANILLA & PINEAPPLE VODKA

½ OUNCE MELON LIQUEUR

3 OUNCES PINEAPPLE JUICE

½ OUNCE FRESH LIME JUICE

½ CUP VANILLA ICE CREAM (SEE NOTE)

1 EDIBLE ORCHID, FOR GARNISH (OPTIONAL)

In a blender, combine the melon chunks, vodka, melon liqueur, pineapple juice, lime juice, ice cream, and 1½ cups of ice. Blend until smooth, then pour into a footed pilsner or hurricane glass. Stab the remaining melon wedge with a drink umbrella and place across the top of the glass with an edible orchid, if desired. Serve with a straw.

> **NOTE:** You can use fat-free frozen yogurt instead of ice cream for a lighter version of the cocktail.

LONO

In traditional Hawaiian culture, Lono is the god of fertility and peace. This cocktail earned its name after not one but two couples told me that they conceived their first child after downing a few of these potent concoctions.

3 OUNCES HULA HUT HULA JUICE SPICED COCONUT RUM (OR A MIX OF 1½ OUNCES COCONUT RUM AND 1½ OUNCES LIGHT RUM)

½ OUNCE FRANGELICO OR OTHER HAZELNUT LIQUEUR

3 OUNCES MANGO NECTAR

2 OUNCES COCO LÓPEZ OR OTHER CREAM OF COCONUT

¼ BANANA

¼ OUNCE DARK RUM

WHIPPED CREAM

1 OUNCE SHREDDED COCONUT

In a blender, combine the rum, Frangelico, mango nectar, cream of coconut, banana, and 1½ cups of ice. Blend on high until smooth. Fill a footed pilsner or hurricane glass with crushed ice, then pour in the cocktail. Float the dark rum on top. Top with whipped cream and a sprinkle of shredded coconut.

PLEASE DON'T TAKE THE TIKI MUGS

According to many reports, tiki mugs are the second most stolen novelty item in bars, right behind the shiny copper mugs used for Moscow Mules. The Hula Hut doesn't serve drinks in tiki mugs, but bartenders around the globe should keep their eyes on their decorative mugs and even tiki bowls after serving them to patrons, who may want more than just a dazzling, delicious drink. These iconic glazed ceramic vessels with evil or funny faces make for great collectible souvenirs in the home bar, especially if they're vintage tiki mugs from historic Hawaiian and Polynesian restaurants and bars. At the height of the tiki craze, the two leading manufacturers of treasured tiki mugs and bowls were Orchids of Hawaii and Otagiri Mercantile Company. Other rare vessels that command high prices today include tiki mugs that resemble Easter Island moai, and Trader Vic's Mai Tai Joe mug, commonly known as the Suffering Bastard, named after a cocktail of the same name. Most tiki-themed restaurants and bars serve tropical libations from recently produced tiki mugs and bowls. Nevertheless, keep an eye out!

TOASTED COCONUT

SERVES 2

Hold on to your coconuts, this cocktail is a knockout! The scent of cinnamon adds a feeling of calm, but don't let your guard down: the 151 rum packs some serious punch!

3 OUNCES CARIBBEAN
COMFORT INFUSION
(PAGE 29)

1½ OUNCES AMARETTO

1 OUNCE 151 RUM

3 OUNCES COCO LÓPEZ OR
OTHER CREAM OF COCONUT

4 OUNCES ORANGE JUICE

2 OUNCES PINEAPPLE JUICE

WHIPPED CREAM

2 TABLESPOONS TOASTED
COCONUT FLAKES (SEE NOTE)

2 ORANGE WHEELS,
FOR GARNISH

In a blender, combine the Caribbean Comfort Infusion, amaretto, rum, cream of coconut, orange juice, pineapple juice, and 3 cups of ice. Blend on high until smooth, then divide between two small hurricane glasses. Top with whipped cream and a sprinkle of coconut flakes. Garnish each glass with an orange wheel and serve with a straw.

> **NOTE:** Most grocery stores carry toasted coconut flakes. If you can't find them, here's how to make your own: Preheat the oven to 400°F. Sprinkle a thin layer of shredded coconut— found in the baking section of most grocery stores—evenly on a large cookie sheet. Place the sheet on the top rack and toast for 8 to 12 minutes or until the coconut turns golden brown. Be sure to keep an eye on it while it's baking so it doesn't burn. Let cool to room temperature, transfer to a container with a lid, and store in a cool, dry place for up to a week.

BLOODY PARADISE

When you think tiki, you probably don't think Bloody Marys, but the recipes in this chapter all have a delicious tropical twist. After all, who doesn't love paradise? Every Saturday and Sunday at noon, the Hula Hut presents a spectacular Bloody Mary bar. It offers a delicious opportunity for guests to get creative while enjoying a delicious cocktail. We stage a variety of tomato juices and blends, including heirloom tomato, Clamato, V8, and Zing Zang (a New Orleans favorite). We also feature more than twenty different hot sauces and spices, like Slap Ya Mama, Bubba's Butt Blaster, Old Bay, and a collection of curries. Mason jars contain an array of condiments from horseradish pickles and stuffed olives to okra and pickled garlic scapes (the curly flower stalks of garlic plants)—all from the Montauk Farmers Market. You can also have your drink and eat it too by adding fresh jumbo shrimp, crispy bacon, chilled crab claws, or vibrant caprese skewers. The sky's the limit when it comes to Bloody Marys, so have fun setting up your own Bloody Mary bar for your guests. It gives them a great chance to interact, and they'll love it.

BLOODY MANGO

Did you know that mango is the most popular fruit in the world? This tropical symbol of love is available year-round. According to the National Mango Board, the majority of mangoes sold in America come from Mexico, Peru, Ecuador, Brazil, Guatemala, and Haiti. Varieties of the fruit include the Ataulfo, Francis, Haden, Keitt, Kent, and Tommy Atkins—so there's a mango for everyone.

2 OUNCES VODKA

4 OUNCES TOMATO JUICE

3 OUNCES MANGO NECTAR

⅛ TEASPOON FRESH
LEMON JUICE

⅛ TEASPOON SRIRACHA

1 MANGO SPEAR,
FOR GARNISH

Fill a Collins glass with ice. Add the vodka, tomato juice, mango nectar, lemon juice, and sriracha. Pour the mixture into a shaker, then return the mixture to the glass. Repeat. Garnish with the fresh mango spear for a pop of color and a healthy snack while you sip your drink.

BLOODY PINEAPPLE

SERVES 1

This bloody is definitely unique—it's not even close to what you'd expect in a Bloody Mary. The smokiness of the mezcal and the scent of the curry will hit you before the first sip, then the sweet sensation of pineapple and the cool lime create an interesting tropical combination that's easy to enjoy.

1 OUNCE PREMIUM SILVER RUM

1 OUNCE DOS HOMBRES MEZCAL

4 OUNCES V8 JUICE

2 OUNCES PINEAPPLE JUICE

¼ OUNCE FRESH LIME JUICE

⅛ TEASPOON CURRY POWDER

3 OR 4 DASHES HOT SAUCE (SEE NOTE)

1 PINEAPPLE WEDGE, FOR GARNISH

Fill a Collins glass with ice. Add the rum, mezcal, V8, pineapple juice, lime juice, curry powder, and hot sauce. Pour the mixture into a shaker, then return it to the glass. Garnish with the pineapple wedge.

NOTE: Every hot sauce is different. For this recipe I prefer Texas Pete. It's fine to use another brand, but I prefer one with a prominent pepper and cayenne flavor.

BLOODY THAILAND

The surprising flavor of peanuts in this Bloody Mary offers an unexpected yet interestingly pleasant twist that will leave your guests wanting more.

2 OUNCES CUCUMBER
VODKA (PAGE 32)

4 OUNCES TOMATO JUICE

1 OUNCE BANGKOK PADANG
PEANUT SAUCE (SEE NOTE)

¾ OUNCE CUCUMBER,
CILANTRO & JALAPEÑO
PUREE (PAGE 23)

¼ OUNCE FRESH LIME JUICE

¼ TEASPOON SRIRACHA

1 CUCUMBER WHEEL,
FOR GARNISH

Fill a Collins glass with ice. Add the vodka, tomato juice, peanut sauce, puree, lime juice, and sriracha. Pour the mixture into a shaker, then return it to the glass. Repeat, then garnish with the cucumber wheel.

NOTE: Peanut sauce is available in the international foods aisle at most grocery stores.

GINGER ISLAND BLOODY

Like the Bloody Thailand (page 139), the lemongrass and ginger in this delightful cocktail will also conjure images of Thailand, but in a deliciously different way. The combination of sweetness and spice with just a hint of earthy, tangy soy flavor gives this bloody what I like to call a Pacific Rim twist.

2 OUNCES HULA HUT LÉ HUKILAU LEMONGRASS & GINGER VODKA

3 OUNCES TOMATO JUICE

2 OUNCES LYNN'S LEMONADE (PAGE 32)

1 DASH SOY SAUCE

⅛ TEASPOON FRESHLY GROUND BLACK PEPPER

1 SPRIG DILL, FOR GARNISH

1 LEMON WHEEL, FOR GARNISH

Fill a Collins glass with ice. Add the vodka, tomato juice, lemonade, soy sauce, and black pepper. Pour the mixture into a shaker, then return it to the glass. Repeat. Garnish with the dill sprig and lemon wheel.

MAMA FIORITA'S BLOODY CAPRESE

SERVES 1

My loving grandma Fiorita taught me the art of combining flavors and the importance of putting passion into everything I do. Whenever I asked her for a recipe, she said, "I don't know, you have to watch me." In true Italian form, she used a pinch of this and a dash of that. A Sunday favorite featured fresh tomato, mozzarella, and basil drizzled with aged balsamic as an appetizer before the ten courses that followed. This drink, a cocktail and appetizer in one, pays tribute to my dear grandmother.

JUICE OF ½ LEMON

2½ OUNCES CUCUMBER CHILE VODKA (PAGE 30)

4 OUNCES TOMATO JUICE

½ TEASPOON OLD BAY SEASONING

¼ TEASPOON CELERY SALT

¼ TEASPOON FRESHLY GROUND BLACK PEPPER

1 SUNGOLD CHERRY TOMATO, CUT INTO THIRDS, FOR GARNISH

1 (1-INCH) MOZZARELLA BALL OR CUBE, HALVED, FOR GARNISH

1 FRESH BASIL LEAF, FOR GARNISH

½ TEASPOON AGED BALSAMIC VINEGAR

Strain the lemon juice into a Collins glass filled with ice. Add the vodka, tomato juice, Old Bay, celery salt, and pepper. Pour the mixture into a shaker, then return it to the glass. Stab the tomato and mozzarella pieces with a bamboo skewer, and drizzle the vinegar on the mozzarella. Lay the garnish across the top of the glass and add the basil leaf.

PINEAPPLE SAGE BLOODY

SERVES 1

The addition of ground sage beautifully balances this cocktail, mellowing and blending the pepper and creating an extremely smooth flavor.

2 OUNCES DOS HOMBRES MEZCAL

3 OUNCES V8 JUICE

2 OUNCES PINEAPPLE JUICE

¼ OUNCE FRESH LEMON JUICE

¼ TEASPOON GROUND SAGE

2 OR 3 DASHES HOT SAUCE (SEE NOTE)

1 PINEAPPLE WEDGE, FOR GARNISH

1 SPRIG SAGE, FOR GARNISH

Fill a Collins glass with ice. Add the mezcal, V8, pineapple juice, lemon juice, sage, and hot sauce. Pour the mixture into a shaker, then return it to the glass. Repeat. Garnish with the pineapple wedge and sprig of sage.

NOTE: Every hot sauce is different. For this recipe I prefer Texas Pete. It's fine to use another brand, but ideally you want one with a flavor profile that tastes bold, peppery, and warm.

SEA CANDY BLOODY

SERVES 1

This cocktail can be labor intensive, but it's definitely worth the time and effort. One sip and you'll taste why. Now you can have your drink and eat it, too! This drink is garnished with a skewer of scallops, or "sea candy," as the fishermen in Montauk call them.

2 OUNCES VODKA

4 OUNCES CLAMATO JUICE

2 OUNCES MANGO NECTAR

¼ TEASPOON FRESH LEMON JUICE

¼ TEASPOON SOY SAUCE

A FEW SMALL SEA SCALLOPS ON A SKEWER (SEE NOTE), FOR GARNISH

Fill a Collins glass with ice. Add the vodka, Clamato, mango nectar, lemon juice, and soy sauce. Pour the mixture into a shaker, then return it to the glass. Repeat. Garnish with the sea candy scallop skewer and dive in!

NOTE: For a simpler version of this cocktail, you can substitute a lemon wedge for the scallop skewer.

CLASSICS & TWISTS

My father's philosophy is "If it's not broke, don't fix it." Sorry, Dad, but inspiration lies everywhere. These classic recipes are amazing, but nothing beats some good old-fashioned experimentation to update the classics. In this next chapter, you'll find recipes for some of history's most iconic tiki cocktails along with my interpretations of them that have what I like to call a Pacific Rim twist. Never be afraid to experiment with different flavors to create your own signature cocktails.

MAI TAI

Prohibition pushed American cocktail culture east to Europe and also south into the Caribbean. Ernest Gantt spent time with his rum-running grandfather in Haiti and Cuba and then helped launch what became full-blown tiki culture by opening Don the Beachcomber Cafe in Hollywood, California. (He later changed his name to Donn Beachcomber and then Donn Beach.) Several years before World War II began, Victor Bergeron came across the Don the Beachcomber bar and realized that the idea had legs. Bergeron—later known as Trader Vic—helped spread tiki culture by founding the famous Trader Vic's chain. Both men claimed credit for inventing this cocktail, and they fought over it for years. In the Tahitian language, *maitai* means "good," so next time you want a good drink, order a mai tai and raise your glass to both Gantt and Bergeron.

1 OUNCE LIGHT RUM

½ OUNCE CURAÇAO

½ OUNCE ORGEAT (SEE NOTE)

½ OUNCE FRESH LIME JUICE

1 OUNCE DARK RUM

1 MARASCHINO CHERRY, FOR GARNISH

1 ORANGE WHEEL, FOR GARNISH (OPTIONAL)

Fill a cocktail shaker with ice. Add the light rum, curaçao, orgeat, and lime juice. Shake for about 10 seconds, then strain into a large rocks glass filled with crushed ice. Float the dark rum on top and garnish with the maraschino cherry and an orange slice, if you like.

> **NOTE:** Orgeat syrup is a sweet almond syrup with hints of orange flower water.

THE FAMOUS MAI TAI

Everyone has heard of the mai tai, but did you know this legendary cocktail comes with its fair share of trivia and controversy? For instance, the drink that put tiki on the map isn't the mai tai at all but the Zombie. (More about that later.) Not until Hawai'i became a state and the Boeing 747 went into service in 1959 did the mai tai begin to take off; it was first attested as an English word for the drink a couple of years later. But did Ernest Gantt or Vic Bergeron introduce it? Today hundreds of variant recipes exist for the mai tai because back in the day the original was so top secret that everyone decided to invent their own version of it. Regardless of who claims ownership, one thing's for certain: the mai tai is delicious, appreciated, and enjoyed in all its various forms.

SWING TAI

This is my twist on the classic mai tai. It might not seem at first that the ingredients create a drastic change in taste from the original, but the amaretto, Cointreau, and mango nectar beautifully balance this drink, creating a delicious contemporary cocktail.

1½ OUNCES LIGHT RUM

¼ OUNCE AMARETTO

¼ OUNCE COINTREAU

1 OUNCE MANGO NECTAR

2 OUNCES PINEAPPLE JUICE

⅓ OUNCE FRESH LIME JUICE

1 DASH GRENADINE

¼ OUNCE DARK RUM

1 DRUNKEN PINEAPPLE WEDGE, FOR GARNISH

1 TRAVERSE CITY CHERRY BOMB (PAGE 13), FOR GARNISH

Fill a cocktail shaker with ice. Add the light rum, amaretto, Cointreau, mango nectar, pineapple juice, lime juice, and grenadine. Shake for about 5 seconds, then strain into a large rocks glass filled with crushed ice. Garnish with the pineapple wedge and cherry.

OLD-FASHIONED

SERVES 1

This legendary cocktail—created in Louisville, Kentucky, according to some—always takes me back to my younger days. My parents hosted cocktail parties in the yard during warm summer nights. Upstairs, my cousins and I, supposedly asleep, could hear the sounds of laughter and music playing all night long. My father, a lobsterman, owned a bar and made my mother her favorite cocktail, the old-fashioned. The classic recipe calls for bourbon and isn't strictly a tiki drink, although the prevalence of oranges and cherries in modern versions helps give it a tropical twist. My mother still prefers hers made with Scotch, but you can use rye or any other whiskey you like. It's up to you!

2 TEASPOONS SIMPLE SYRUP

2 ORANGE WHEELS

2 MARASCHINO CHERRIES

2 DASHES BITTERS

1½ OUNCES MAKER'S MARK, BULLEIT, OR OTHER PREMIUM BOURBON

In a large rocks glass, combine the simple syrup, 1 of the orange wheels, 1 of the cherries, and the bitters. Muddle the fruit to release the juices and to blend the syrup and bitters. Fill the glass with ice, then add the bourbon. Garnish with the remaining orange wheel and maraschino cherry.

ISLAND FASHIONED

SERVES 1

Every classic needs a Caribbean or Pacific Rim twist. The cinnamon, nutmeg, and mango nectar in this tropical version of the old-fashioned provide a soothing remedy for a sore throat as well as the perfect sipping cocktail after dinner.

1 MANDARIN ORANGE

3 OUNCES MANGO NECTAR

½ OUNCE LIGHT SIMPLE SYRUP (PAGE 22)

⅛ TEASPOON FRESHLY GRATED NUTMEG

⅛ TEASPOON GROUND SAIGON CINNAMON

2½ OUNCES MAKER'S MARK OR BULLEIT BOURBON

1 MANDARIN ORANGE WHEEL, FOR GARNISH

1 ROCK CANDY SKEWER, FOR GARNISH (OPTIONAL)

1 BOUDREAUX'S BOURBON CHERRY BOMB (PAGE 13), FOR GARNISH (OPTIONAL)

Peel the orange and place three sections in a rocks glass. Add the mango nectar, simple syrup, nutmeg, and cinnamon. Muddle to release the juice of the orange and to blend the nectar, syrup, and spices. Fill the glass with ice, add the bourbon, and transfer to a cocktail shaker. Shake for about 5 seconds, then pour the cocktail back into the glass.

Garnish with the mandarin orange wheel. Lay the rock candy skewer atop the glass and finish with the cherry, if desired.

PISCO SOUR

In the mid-1600s, King Philip IV of Spain levied taxes on wine production in Peru, so winemakers turned to moonshining by distilling their grapes in large copper vats. The Peruvians named their new creation after the Port of Pisco, where the liquor was exported (quickly!). Today Peruvians refer to Pisco as their native spirit, which is now made in vineyards along the southwestern coast of Peru using different grape varietals. It's still produced in copper vats and often crafted in small batches.

2 OUNCES PISCO PORTÓN

1 OUNCE SIMPLE SYRUP

1 OUNCE FRESH LIME JUICE

1 OUNCE EGG WHITE

3 DASHES ANGOSTURA BITTERS

Combine the Pisco, simple syrup, lime juice, and egg white in a blender. Blend on high for about 15 seconds. Add about 5 ice cubes and pulse the blender five times. Strain into a chilled coupe and add the bitters.

SWEET BASIL PISCO

SERVES 1

At the Hula Hut, we shake all sorts of drinks to aerate the mixture, thus "waking up" the cocktail. For this drink, shake hard and quick. You're not trying to rock your drink to sleep, so shake it with energy! When shaking, remember to aim the top of your shaker away from your guests. That way, if a dreaded mishap occurs, the liquid shoots behind you instead of hosing down the person in front of you. This deliciously fresh cocktail is amazing on a hot summer day with seafood or salads.

2 OUNCES PISCO

½ OUNCE ST-GERMAIN OR OTHER ELDERFLOWER LIQUEUR

2 OUNCES WATERMELON & BASIL PUREE (PAGE 27)

¾ OUNCE FRESH LEMON JUICE

1 WATERMELON WEDGE, FOR GARNISH

1 SPRIG BASIL, FOR GARNISH

In a cocktail shaker, combine the Pisco, St-Germain, puree, and lemon juice. Add several ice cubes and shake for about 5 seconds. Strain into a large chilled rocks glass filled halfway with crushed ice. Garnish with the watermelon wedge and float the basil sprig on top.

SAKETINI

Sake, an alcohol made from rice, is a favorite in Japan. It's often aged for about six months, during which time it undergoes a fermentation process that resembles brewing beer more than making wine. The more polished or clean the rice, the higher the grade of sake. There are many sakes on the market. Some are designed to be consumed chilled and others consumed warm. When in doubt, select a middle-grade sake, especially for this classic cocktail, which was introduced in the 1960s.

2½ OUNCES GIN

1½ TEASPOONS SAKE

1 COCKTAIL OLIVE,
FOR GARNISH

Combine the gin and sake in a cocktail shaker filled with ice. Shake for about 10 seconds, strain into a chilled martini glass, and garnish with a cocktail olive.

CUCUMBER SORBET SAKETINI

SERVES 1

You're going to love the fresh ginger, cold lemon sorbet, and fresh cucumber in my Pacific twist on the Matsuda San classic. It's so refreshing.

3 CUCUMBER SLICES, ABOUT ⅛ INCH THICK

¼ OUNCE FRESH LEMON JUICE

½ OUNCE LIGHT SIMPLE SYRUP (PAGE 22)

2 OUNCES HULA HUT LĒ HUKILAU LEMONGRASS & GINGER VODKA

½ OUNCE DRY SAKE

⅛ TEASPOON MINCED FRESH GINGER

1 SCOOP OF LEMON SORBET, ABOUT 2 INCHES IN DIAMETER

1 SPRIG LEMON VERBENA, FOR GARNISH

In a cocktail shaker, combine the cucumber, lemon juice, and simple syrup. Muddle well. Add the vodka, sake, ginger, and 1 cup of ice. Shake vigorously for about 10 seconds. Scoop the sorbet into a chilled martini glass. Strain the cocktail over the sorbet and garnish with the sprig of lemon verbena.

SCORPION BOWL

SERVES 2 TO 4

Originating in Honolulu in the 1930s, the Scorpion Bowl traditionally is served in a communal volcano bowl, which has a raised cup in the center to hold the overproof liquor, which is ignited to simulate an erupting volcano. Some versions of the bowl made specifically for this cocktail feature scorpions on the rim, onto which you can affix various garnishes such as fresh cherries or pineapple wedges. There are many versions of this festive cocktail, so it's hard to say exactly what the original recipe contained—but I can tell you that it's fun to try them all!

2 OUNCES GIN

2 OUNCES LIGHT RUM

2 OUNCES TITO'S VODKA

1 OUNCE 151 RUM

2 OUNCES GRENADINE

12 OUNCES ORANGE JUICE

3 OUNCES FRESH LEMON JUICE

4 PINEAPPLE CHUNKS

8 MARASCHINO CHERRIES

In a large pitcher, combine the gin, light rum, vodka, 151 rum, grenadine, orange juice, lemon juice, pineapple chunks, and cherries. Stir well to blend the flavors. Add 3 cups of crushed ice and transfer to a large scorpion or volcano bowl (see note). Serve with jumbo straws.

NOTE: If you're using a volcano bowl, pour an additional 1 ounce 151 rum into the center cup and carefully set the booze alight.

GEMINI BOWL

SERVES 2 OR MORE

Some people say Scorpios have all the fun, but as a Gemini, I say that's just not true. The third astrological sign in the zodiac is named for the Gemini constellation, which honors Castor and Pollux from ancient Greek myth. After the mortal Castor died, Pollux, his immortal twin, asked to share a portion of his immortality so they could remain together. In later versions of the myth, they appear to sailors as St. Elmo's fire. For my birthday, which falls in mid-June, I like to serve this Gemini variation on the classic Scorpion Bowl. It's festive, delicious, and dangerous at the same time. Don't say I didn't warn you.

2 OUNCES GIN	2 OUNCES FRESH LEMON JUICE
3 OUNCES HULA HUT HULA JUICE SPICED COCONUT RUM	2 OUNCES ORANGE JUICE
2 OUNCES LIGHT RUM	2 OUNCES PINEAPPLE JUICE
2 OUNCES CHINOLA PASSION FRUIT LIQUEUR	4 PINEAPPLE CHUNKS
2 OUNCES VODKA	4 TRAVERSE CITY CHERRY BOMBS (PAGE 13)
2 OUNCES GRENADINE	SUGARCANE PIECES, FOR GARNISH (OPTIONAL)
2 OUNCES MANGO NECTAR	

In a large pitcher, combine the gin, both rums, the Chinola, vodka, grenadine, mango nectar, lemon juice, orange juice, and pineapple juice. Stir well to blend the flavors. Refrigerate for 2 to 3 hours before serving.

When ready to serve, add 3 cups of crushed ice to a large volcano or scorpion bowl. Pour the chilled cocktail into the bowl, then float the pineapple chunks and cherries atop the drink. Garnish with sugarcane, if desired, and serve with straws. (If you're using a volcano bowl, see the note on page 163.)

SINGAPORE SLING

Many recipes claim to be the original Singapore Sling. Chinese bartender Ngiam Tong Boon boasted that he invented the iconic libation in 1915 at the Raffles Hotel in Singapore. The first handwritten recipe disappeared many years ago, and many cocktail buffs dispute the original ingredients. But this is the recipe still served at the Raffles Hotel in Singapore.

1½ OUNCES PREMIUM GIN

1 OUNCE B&B (BÉNÉDICTINE AND BRANDY)

1 OUNCE CHERRY BRANDY

1 OUNCE FRESH LIME JUICE

CLUB SODA, CHILLED

1 DASH ANGOSTURA BITTERS

Fill a cocktail shaker with ice. Add the gin, B&B, cherry brandy, and lime juice. Shake for 5 seconds. Strain into a Collins glass filled with crushed ice and top with club soda and a dash of bitters.

NOTE: The original recipe didn't include a garnish.

SINGAPORE SWING

SERVES 1

I had a bad experience with gin in my early years, as plenty of people have. But after some time, I gave it another shot. (No pun intended.) I started experimenting by adding fresh fruits and syrups to balance the bitterness of the gin, and that's how this twist on the Singapore Sling came about.

1½ OUNCES GIN	1 DASH ANGOSTURA BITTERS
¼ OUNCE CHAMBORD OR OTHER RASPBERRY LIQUEUR	3 OR 4 FRESH RASPBERRIES, RINSED
LYNN'S LEMONADE (PAGE 32)	1 LEMON WHEEL, FOR GARNISH
CHERRY SODA	

Fill a Collins glass with crushed ice. Add the gin and Chambord, then add equal parts lemonade and cherry soda to fill the glass to within ½ inch from the top. Add the bitters.

Float the raspberries atop the drink, garnish with the lemon wheel, and serve with a straw.

ZOMBIE

Donn Beach concocted the classic Zombie in 1939. Heavily guarded by its creator, the original recipe had a limit of two per customer because it made the imbiber feel like, well, you know. Many interpretations of this classic cocktail have appeared over the years, but this one is said to be closest to the original.

1½ OUNCES PUERTO RICAN GOLD RUM

1½ OUNCES JAMAICAN LIGHT RUM

¼ TEASPOON PERNOD

1 TEASPOON GRENADINE

3 OUNCES FRESH GRAPEFRUIT JUICE

1 DASH ANGOSTURA BITTERS

1 TEASPOON SUGAR

½ TEASPOON GROUND CINNAMON

1 OUNCE 151 RUM

1 CHERRY, FOR GARNISH

In a cocktail shaker filled with ice, combine the Puerto Rican and Jamaican rums, Pernod, grenadine, grapefruit juice, bitters, sugar, and cinnamon. Shake for 5 to 10 seconds, then strain into a Collins glass filled with ice. Float the 151 rum on top and garnish with a cherry.

ZYDECO ZOMBIE

SERVES 1

By now you know that there's a warm place in my heart for southern Louisiana and Cajun culture. My version of the iconic Zombie cocktail has a little lagniappe (pronounced *LAN-yap*), a Cajun term meaning "a little something extra." Maybe it's the heat from the hot sauce, or the rum-soaked cherries, but one sip will remind you of a full moon on the bayou.

2½ OUNCES HULA HUT HULA JUICE SPICED COCONUT RUM (OR A MIX OF 1½ OUNCES SPICED RUM AND 1 OUNCE LIGHT RUM)

½ OUNCE DARK RUM

½ OUNCE APRICOT BRANDY

½ OUNCE CANE SYRUP

3 OUNCES GRAPEFRUIT JUICE

½ OUNCE FRESH LIME JUICE

¼ TEASPOON CINNAMON

3 DASHES CRYSTAL OR OTHER LOUISIANA HOT SAUCE

1 DASH ANGOSTURA BITTERS

1 (8- TO 10-INCH) SUGARCANE STALK, FOR GARNISH

1 TRAVERSE CITY CHERRY BOMB (PAGE 13), FOR GARNISH

1 CINNAMON STICK, FOR GARNISH

1 LIME TWIST, FOR GARNISH

In a cocktail shaker filled with ice, combine the coconut rum, dark rum, brandy, cane syrup, grapefruit juice, lime juice, cinnamon, hot sauce, and bitters. Shake for 5 seconds, then strain into a mason jar or glass of your choice filled with ice, leaving 1 inch at the top. Garnish with a sugarcane stalk, cherry, cinnamon stick, and a lime twist. Play some Chubby Carrier and the Bayou Swamp Band, and *laissez les bons temps rouler*!

NOTE: For that extra presentation effect, serve this drink in a pint glass with green LED lights in the base. You can find them online at CoolGlow.com.

ACKNOWLEDGMENTS

Thanks to my incredibly talented coauthor, James O. Fraioli, and to Chris, for his love and invaluable support—thank you for being my rock. Many thanks to Terry Howisey, for being such an invaluable part of Hula Hut Spirits; Bruce and Carol B., for believing in me and supporting this brand; David Mandell, my advisor, cofounder of Bardstown Bourbon company, and CEO and cofounder of the Whiskey House of Kentucky; David Silverman, for your guidance; Kay Peluso; and, last but not least, my wonderful parents, for your love, support, and encouragement.

RECIPE INDEX

Note: Page references in *italics* indicate photographs.

GENERAL INDEX

Note: Page references in *italics* indicate photographs.